Penny Tassoni

REDUCING EDUCATIONAL DISADVANTAGE

A Strategic Approach in the Early Years

Featherstone Education
An imprint of Bloomsbury Publishing Plc

50 Bedford Square	1385 Broadway
London	New York
WC1B 3DP	NY 10018
UK	USA

www.bloomsbury.com

First published 2016

British Library Cataloguing-in-Publication Data
A catalogue record for this book is available from the British Library.

ISBN:
PB 978-1-4729-3299-0
ePub 978-1-4729-3301-0
ePDF 978-1-4729-3300-3

Library of Congress Cataloging-in-Publication Data
A catalog record for this book is available from the Library of Congress.

10 9 8 7 6 5 4 3 2 1

Printed and bound in India by Replika Press Pvt. Ltd.

This book is produced using paper that is made from wood grown in managed, sustainable forests.
It is natural, renewable and recyclable. The logging and manufacturing processes conform to the
environmental regulations of the country of origin.

To view more of our titles please visit www.bloomsbury.com

Acknowledgements

The charts on p105 - 107 are reproduced with kind permission of Kent Community Health
NHS Foundation Trust.

Contents

Contents (contd.)

Closing the gap

Increasingly over the past few years, there has been an understanding that some children, through no fault of their own, are at a disadvantage throughout their educational journey and beyond. Whilst early years settings have always strived to support children's development, the reality is that some children have a measurable advantage over others very early on in life. I dub these children as being 'lucky children'.

The issues around disadvantage are, as we will see, complex, but like most people working in early years, I believe in equality of opportunity and so am keen to explore approaches that may make a difference. As a sector, I am concerned that we are increasingly under pressure by successive governments to become more formal in our approach to early education. I believe that taking this path would be a huge mistake and that instead of supporting children at risk of disadvantage, it would instead create a further divide.

Having dismissed formal learning as a solution, I do however believe that we need to replicate many of the experiences and opportunities that 'lucky' children have. This requires taking a strategic approach that needs some long term planning. In this book, I am hoping to explore strategies, experiences and also activities that will make a developmental difference to children who are at risk of social disadvantage. I have also included a sizeable chapter about how to support children who are bilingual, as statistically these children are more likely to underperform in their first years at school.

As every early years setting is different, as too are children's needs, I am not suggesting a one-size-fits-all approach, but I would urge every setting to reflect carefully on their approach. What works well for children of more affluent families may not always be as effective in supporting the needs of children who are at risk of disadvantage.

Behind the scenes

In order to develop an approach to supporting children at risk of disadvantage, it is worth delving into recent reports and research that surround the issue of social mobility and disadvantage. It is interesting that social mobility and the impact of poverty on children's life chances has been a hot topic for policy makers of all political persuasions. Reports commissioned by both government and other organisations make for poignant reading. They clearly spell out the difference between the 'lucky' children and others whose circumstances are not so fortunate. Thinking carefully about how our practice can support these children is therefore imperative.

Frank Field's report (2010)

One of the flurry of reports that were published within the first year of the coalition government's election in 2010 was 'The Foundation Years: preventing poor children becoming poor adults'. Led by labour MP, Frank Field, at the request of the Prime Minister, it made a clear link to children's later chances and their earliest years. One of the notable comments that he made in his report was in relation to the link between low income and later development. He drew on two pieces of research by Leon Feinstein: 'How early can we predict future educational achievement?' and 'Inequality in the early cognitive development of British children in the early 1970 cohort', and described their 'disturbing' findings as follows:

> *The successes individuals achieve during their adult life can be predicted by the level of cognitive and non cognitive skills they already possess on their first day at school. These differences in skill levels have been noted after as little as 22 months of life, and are shown to widen within the toddler population by the age of five.*

The report contained 24 wide-ranging recommendations which included the importance of focusing services and strategies on children and their families between the ages of 0 and 5 years, dubbed the 'Foundation Years'. Some of the recommendations centred on the importance of parenting, including a recommendation that parenting should be included as part of the school curriculum culminating in a GCSE. Another interesting recommendation was that full-time, graduate-led childcare should be made available for children from low income families from age two.

Graham Allen's report (2011)

Graham Allen's report, 'Early intervention: the next steps' in January 2011 also looked at the link between early years and later development. Many of the conclusions that Graham Allen reached were complementary to those in Frank Field's report, including those around the importance of parenting. Interestingly though, Graham Allen in this and in a subsequent report published in July 2011, focused on the economic as well as the social benefits of early intervention. Of particular note was the recommendation that 'school readiness' should be a focus for the Foundation Years along with regular assessment of children's development with a particular emphasis on emotional and social development.

Dame Clare Tickell's report (2011)

Hard on the heels of Frank Field's and Graham Allen's reports was a review of the EYFS by Dame Clare Tickell, 'The Early Years: Foundations for Life, Health and Learning – an Independent Report on the Early Years Foundation Stage'. Whilst this was not a report solely about children and social disadvantage, its findings dovetailed into those of the previous reports. The report had 46 recommendations, which were widely applauded at the time. They included the importance of upskilling the early years workforce (something that Frank Field had also commented on), the need to introduce a development check between age two and three years, as well as an overhaul of the EYFS to include a focus on three prime areas of development: personal, social and emotional development, communication and language, and physical development.

Language levels and later achievement

The role that early communication and language plays in children's later development is a recurring feature in many of the reports about children at risk of disadvantage. You may find these statistics that ICAN, the communication charity, have compiled from a range of sources, interesting in this respect.

Early language: facts and stats (ICAN 2014)

★ **By 22 months** – a child's language development can predict outcomes at age 26

★ **By ages 3-6 years** – a child's narrative skills are a powerful predictor of literacy skill at 8-12 years

★ **By 4 years** – the difference in the number of words children from disadvantaged backgrounds hear is 19 million

★ **By 5 years** – a child's vocabulary will predict their educational success and outcomes at age 30.

Social mobility

There are several interesting reports and statistics that look at how more affluent families use their resources to advantage their own children. I use the term 'resources' loosely, to mean not just finances, but knowledge about the education system, networks and contacts. Some parents will, for example, go to extra lengths to get their child into a school that is highly rated or will pay for their children to attend 'booster' classes. The effects of this can be seen in outcomes for children. There are several reports that look at this effect including the research brief published by the Sutton Trust in September 2014 entitled 'Extra-curricular inequalities'. This paper looks at how more affluent parents provide both additional educational support, but also more cultural activities for children.

> *Private tuition has obvious benefits, but previous research has also shown that 'softer' cultural experience (cultural capital) and participation in extra-curricular activities like music, dance, and sports can have a positive effect on both educational attainment and career outcomes.*
>
> **The Sutton Trust, (2014)**

'Downward mobility, opportunity hoarding and the 'glass floor' is another similar report published by the Social Mobility and Child Poverty Commission. It looked at the many ways in which affluent parents ensure that their offspring maintain their advantage.

> *Families with greater means at their disposal, financial and otherwise, are assisting their children to accumulate skills, particularly those which are valued in the labour market. We observe this through improvements in cognitive skills (maths especially) by age 10 and a greater likelihood of gaining a degree.*
>
> **Abigail McKnight, Social Mobility and Child Poverty Commission, (2015)**

The Effective Provision of Pre-school Education (EPPE) project

The 'Effective Provision of Pre-School Education Project' was a longitudinal study funded by the then Department of Education and Skills in 1997. It followed a cohort of three-year-olds from a variety of home backgrounds and early years settings, although sadly not childminder settings. It also followed children who did not have pre-school experiences. Since its inception, looking at the impact of early education, it has continued to evolve and has since reported on the cohort of children's progress in their primary and secondary phase of education. Its findings have influenced social and education policy in England, notably the implementation of three-hour session funding for three- and four-year-olds and the focus on engaging parents to support their children at home. As a project it has generated huge amounts of data, but for our purposes, I believe that we should focus on the following key findings:

- High quality pre-school makes a difference
- Home learning environments matter.

High quality pre-schooling makes a difference

The researchers concluded that high quality pre-school experiences have the potential to make a tangible difference to children's later achievement. This is good news in terms of supporting children who are at risk of disadvantage. The research team gave plenty of pointers as to what, in their estimation, made an early years setting of high quality. These include the level of qualification of staff, but also the way in which staff worked with children.

What makes an early years setting high quality?

Findings taken from the EPPE project report.

- Equal balance of adult-initiated to child-initiated activity

> *In effective settings, the balance of who initiated the activities, staff or child, was about equal. Children were encouraged to initiate activities as often as the staff.'*

- High level of sustained interactions during child-initiated activity

> *Similarly, in effective settings the extent to which staff extended child-initiated interactions was important. Almost half of the child initiated episodes which contained intellectual challenge, included interventions from a staff member to extend the child's thinking.*

- Importance of 1:1 or 1:2 adult-child interactions

> *It was found that the most effective settings encourage 'sustained shared thinking' which was most likely to occur when children were interacting 1:1 with an adult or with a single peer partner. It would appear that periods of 'sustained shared thinking' are a necessary pre-requisite for the most effective early years practice.*

Home learning matters

Whilst the EPPE project did find that a mother's educational level is an influence on children's later development, the home learning environment was a key factor on children's attainment. The since well-quoted phrase, 'What parents do with their children is more important than who parents are' sums up the importance of how parents engaged with their children.

> *There are a range of activities that parents undertake with pre-school children which have a positive effect on their development. For example, reading with the child, teaching songs and nursery rhymes, painting and drawing, playing with letters and numbers, visiting the library, teaching the alphabet and numbers, taking children on visits and creating regular opportunities for them to play with their friends at home, were all associated with higher intellectual and social/behavioural scores.*

Gender

One feature of the EPPE's examination into the home learning environment that is less reported, but I feel could be significant, is around gender and learning activities.

> *There is evidence that overall parenting styles vary for girls and boys. Parents were more likely to engage in specific kinds of learning activities with girls.*

The EPPE project also noted that better outcomes were associated when there was a strong partnership with parents.

> *The most effective settings shared child-related information between parents and staff, and parents were often involved in decision making about their child's learning programme. There were more intellectual gains for children in centres that encouraged high levels of parental involvement.*

Summary

As we have seen, there are many reports and research papers looking at early childhood development and the links to social disadvantage. It seems clear to me that if we are to make a difference in early years, we need to focus carefully on some key areas and ways of working with children and of course their parents. It is evidence taken from the range of reports that I have used to make suggestions and to be the basis of each of the chapters in this book.

Amongst the EPPE project's findings, for example, there are several clues as to ways in which we might effectively work with children at risk of disadvantage, including the need for adult-initiated activity and one to one interactions. From the reports into social mobility, we might pull out the importance of experiences and opportunities. In addition, the correlations found in several reports between vocabulary and later achievement also highlight the significance of working on children's communication and language skills. Finally, it is clear that parents are a major piece of the jigsaw puzzle and so finding ways to support them in their role as parents and to involve them in their children's early education must also be a focus for our work.

Chapter 1

Working in partnership with parents

If we are to find ways of closing the gap and supporting children at risk of disadvantage, engaging with parents is essential.

Parents are invaluable for their children. They not only provide long term emotional security, but they also help to orient children in terms of aspiration, values and beliefs. Parents are also able to act as springboards when it comes to their children's early development in a way that is unique. When parents and early years settings are able to make strong connections and work in partnership with each other, outcomes for children are favourable. This is because early years practitioners and parents have different skill and knowledge sets, and bringing them together is a potent force.

There are plenty of useful books, articles and resources available for practitioners wishing to learn more about parent–practitioner relationships (see Bibliography and further reading, page 183), and so in this chapter I have decided to focus instead on some of the issues and practical strategies worth considering in the context of supporting children at risk of disadvantage. I use the term, 'parent' loosely to refer to any adult who is a primary carer in a child's life, which may include, for example, step-parents, grandparents and foster carers.

> *What parents do with their children is more important than who parents are*
>
> **(EPPE Project report, see Introduction page 9)**

In the report quoted above, Kathy Sylva et al were able to demonstrate that the effect of a strong home learning environment was tangible even when children were six or seven years old.

Unfortunately, some parents remain unaware of their own significance in their children's development. Whilst they may recognise the emotional connection between them and the physical care that they offer, they may not realise the impact that they can have on all areas of their children's development.

It could be argued that government policies have not always helped in this respect. The recent focus in England, for example, has been to encourage parents to leave their children in early years settings at increasingly earlier ages. I would argue that this sends out an underlying message that early years settings are more capable than parents. This is simply not true. Although parents may not have the child development knowledge base that we as professionals have, their relationship and hence influence on their children's potential development is extraordinarily precious. Even though there are some parents who struggle in their parenting role for a number of reasons, the overall majority of parents are there for their children and have their best interests at heart. It is therefore up to us to find ways of engaging with parents so that together we can collaborate.

Understanding the factors that may impact on parental engagement

There are many reasons why some parents feel connected to early years settings whereas others do not. Ideally, we should be trying to find ways of engaging with all parents, as the benefits for children are significant where there is some level of parental involvement with a setting. A good starting point is to consider some of the invisible barriers that may prevent parents from being able to engage with us.

Time constraints

Whilst the stereotype is that children who are at risk of educational disadvantage have parents who are not in work, this is not necessarily the case. Some parents work long hours and often juggle more than one job. They may work shifts and/or have a range of caring responsibilities. Some parents will also be dropping off their children on the way to work or picking them up just as the setting is about to close. Time can therefore prevent them from carrying out those typical activities linked to parental engagement, such as attending meetings, contributing to observations and reading home-setting information. Settings that recognise that time is a barrier, work with parents to find flexible ways of helping them to be connected to the setting. These may include using websites and social media as well as e-mails, phone calls and home-setting books for sharing more personal information.

Working parents can find it hard to engage with a setting.

Reflection points

- What methods do you use to help parents for whom time is a potential barrier to their engagement?

- How do you involve parents in finding solutions?

- Are you flexible in your approach to communicating and sharing information?

Gender

We know that men are significant role models for young boys. Research has shown the impact that fathers sharing books can have on their son's interest and attainment in reading. For girls too, fathers are important. Their relationship with their father is often a template for their later relationships with men. All men are different of course, but many couples will also report that there is something special about the way that fathers play with their children. They often say that fathers will play for longer, are more patient and are less risk-averse, allowing children to be more independent. The message is fairly clear – dads matter!

It is therefore important to think carefully about how we welcome and engage with dads, grandfathers or other men who act as parents. Some men report that they feel uncomfortable when they come into settings, especially if they are with the child's mother. They often use the term 'spare part' to describe their experience. The key person or other members of staff may address comments at the mother rather than encouraging the father to contribute. Therefore it is important to help fathers understand how important they are to their children. There are many ways of doing this. Some settings, for example, have dad's groups or plan drop-in times when dads can engage in activities that they feel comfortable doing. When men pick up their children, some settings have members of staff who take time to greet them and explain how their child is benefitting from their involvement.

Reflection points

- How do you help fathers to feel welcome when they come into your setting?

- Do you create specific opportunities for fathers to participate in their child's learning and development?

Own experiences of education

Many people working in education are 'signed up' believers of the value of education. In some cases, their own parents, as well as previous generations of their family have had success within the education system and so are great supporters of it. In addition, people who have benefitted from education are also likely to find the physical buildings, routines and expectations comfortable and can relax in them.

For some of the parents that we work with, none of the above is true. They may not share our beliefs about the value of education, and their own experiences of it may have been far from positive. At best, they may have found education an irrelevance and just something that had to be endured. At worst, some parents have experienced humiliation, intimidation or bullying from their peers, and so coming into an education environment is a very uncomfortable experience.

Reflection points

- Do you actively look for signs that parents are feeling uncomfortable in the setting, e.g. body language or eye contact? How do you acknowledge this?

- Do you recognise that some parents may take some time before they can fully engage with you?

A welcoming environment can help parents feel more at ease.

Language levels

Many settings today have families whose home language is different from that of the setting. For some parents, their own level of the setting's language may be a barrier to their engagement. They may not feel confident about asking questions or sharing information. They may also be concerned that they will not be able to understand what is being said to them. Some parents may therefore ask another family member to liaise with the early years setting or they may keep their interactions to a minimum. Where conversations have taken place, they may not want to show that they have not understood.

Settings that work well with parents who are not fluent users of English, employ a variety of methods to facilitate communication, including technology such as online translation, magic pens as well as translating sensitive materials using qualified translators.

Differing educational expectations

Whilst we may believe that learning through a play-based approach is important for children's development, some parents may believe that children should be formally taught from an early age. On the other hand, there may be some parents who believe that the education system is too formal and oppose any form of assessment, including the two-year-old check that is statutory in England. There are many reasons why parents may have differing expectations and these may include the type of education system that they experienced as a child.

Reflection points

- How do you facilitate communication with parents who may not be users of English?

- How do you ensure that parents have understood key information, such as policies relating to emergencies?

- How do you help parents feel welcome and valued as users of another language? Do you greet them in their own language?

Reflection points

- How do you explore with parents the educational aims of your setting?

- Do you listen to the parents' views and acknowledge these respectfully?

Literacy levels

Many settings underestimate how many adults have difficulties or confidence issues with reading and writing. Statistics on literacy rates vary, but according to the Literacy Trust, around 16 percent of adults in England are likely to have difficulties, with writing in particular being a challenge. (Literacy Trust, 'How many illiterate adults are there in England?') As many early years settings ask parents to read policies, fill in forms and contribute to learning journeys or other assessments, this can be very problematic for parents. Some parents therefore avoid going into settings in case they are put on the spot and asked to read or write something. Others will keep to a minimum the amount they write on forms, observations or in letters. This may lead some early years settings to the conclusion that parents are not interested.

Settings that are aware of potential difficulties arising from literacy levels are careful not to make any assumptions about parents' abilities. They may for example, routinely offer to write things for parents and will often paraphrase policies or written information. They may also make it easier for parents by not using 'jargon' in written information and also by keeping the length of sentences short. In addition, they make it easy for parents to admit that they find aspects of literacy challenging by saying things such as, 'We know that not everyone loves writing and so if you want, I can write it for you'.

Creating a welcoming environment that supports positive parental engagement

There is no magic formula to creating a welcoming environment. Although it is partly about the physical environment, it is mainly about the atmosphere created by the people who are in it. The test of whether an environment is welcoming is what parents feel and say about it.

The personal touch

A good start when creating a welcoming environment is to remember that each and every parent is first and foremost an individual – they just happen to have children. Whilst we come together in early years settings because of their children, strong working relationships need to have an element of recognising parents as unique individuals too. Small things such as referring to parents by their own name rather than 'Marty's mother' or 'Rajeet's dad' demonstrate this. In settings where there are strong partnerships with parents, there is often an injection of the personal into the setting-parent relationship. A parent who is a known fan of a football team will be congratulated if the team wins, or if a family has come back from holiday, parents will be asked if they had a good time. Although there is of course a professional balance to be struck, it is important that parents feel that we are approachable and 'human'.

Meeting and greeting

First impressions count and so a welcoming setting focuses on how parents are acknowledged and physically welcomed into the setting. Smiles count for a lot, as well as some sort of greeting that is appropriate. In some cases, a parent may not come with an appointment and indeed it may not be a particularly convenient time. This is the true test of an 'open door' policy. An apology and an indication of where a parent can wait, or in the case of a group care setting, a quick transfer to another adult are all ways of avoiding parents feeling that they are not welcome or are a nuisance.

Greetings are an important part of making parents feel at ease.

Signage

The signs that are put up in any setting can unwittingly be barriers for parents. Too many signs can feel threatening to those parents who find reading difficult, and the tone of signs can also be off-putting. Think carefully about signs that begin with, 'Don't' as these can create a negative atmosphere. Interestingly, many organisations such as restaurants and supermarkets find ways of turning messages such as, 'Don't smoke here' into positives such as, 'This is a non-smoking zone'.

On the other hand, good use of signs can create a positive ambiance. Some settings will put up a sign saying, 'Have a good weekend' or will mark a child's birthday or significant family event with a sign.

Displays

Some of the most physically welcoming spaces use displays effectively. There is a place for displays that have relevant and up to date information that parents will find genuinely interesting, but some of the most appealing displays focus on the 'best bits' of the setting. This might be artwork or photographs and maybe, in this era of technology, film clips and digital photographs.

Practicalities

Welcoming environments have also addressed some of the practicalities that can hinder parents coming into settings or staying to talk. Practicalities include: somewhere for buggies to go, somewhere to sit if parents/carers need to wait and appropriate toys or books for older children who may with them. For many parents, being with other parents is a huge support and so a welcoming environment recognises this.

Reflection points

- Have you ever asked for feedback from parents/visitors about how welcoming they found your setting when they first came in?

- At first glance, does the visual environment look attractive and welcoming?

- Do you always warmly acknowledge parents?

- Do you have an open door policy and how does this work in reality?

- Do you have somewhere for parents to wait or to engage with each other?

Parents need to feel that their child will be happy when they leave them.

The importance of the key person role in fostering relationships with parents

In many ways, the day to day business of creating and maintaining strong relationships begins and ends with the child's key person. Although everyone in the setting needs to play a role in making parents feel welcome, it is the strength of the key person relationship that makes a difference as to whether or not parents feel at ease in the setting.

It is hard to overestimate the benefits of a strong key person-parent benefit. From the children's perspective, it makes moving from one adult to another a pleasant transition as they can sense the warmth between the adults. This warmth also facilitates strong communication between parents and the key person. It means that comments or questions can be asked without fear of their being 'taken the wrong way'. It means that if either the parent or key person wants to share ideas or concerns about the child's development, behaviour or progress, this can be done easily.

A strong relationship is also essential if the key person is to be able to make suggestions as to how parents may support their child's learning at home. This is because when a key person knows a parent well, it is easier to make relevant as well as realistic suggestions of things that might benefit the child. The key person will know how and when to make the suggestion too. This personal approach is far more effective than signs or posters in a setting. From a parent's perspective, suggestions from a key person that one likes and respects are more likely to be considered, knowing that they are made with the child's interests at heart.

We should never forget that parents also have their own expertise that we should encourage them to share. Not only are they experts in their children's lives, they are also experts about how well our setting provides for them. Where relationships are strong, we can learn from parents about how we might improve the way we work with them, which may include the information we provide.

The importance of settling in

A smooth transition whereby children are happy for their parents to leave is essential. Children will only benefit from the play and opportunities on offer if they are relaxed and feel emotionally secure. This comes from children having a strong key person relationship (see Chapter 5). For many parents, leaving their child with someone that they do not know is a huge hurdle and one that we must not underestimate. Nature did not intend for parents to leave their young offspring with strangers, and so settling in is a three-way process resulting in the child, the key person and the parents becoming comfortable with each other.

Getting to know each other

Parents will always find it easier to leave their children with us when they feel that they know us a little and also that they can see that their child is comfortable with us. This needs to be the focus of the settling in process which might start off as a home visit, a chat during a 'stay and play' session or at a meeting.

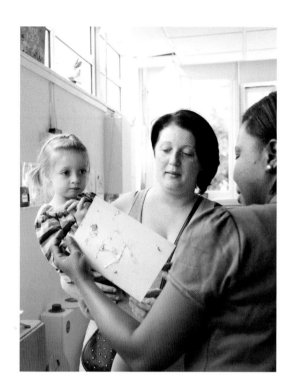

A good starting point is to make sure that when you first meet parents that you share a little information about yourself. This might include how long you have been working with children and why you enjoy your job, but also a little information that will help parents to relate to you as a person. This might include whether you have children, pets or hobbies (see Tip below). Of course, the personal information that you share needs to be thought through, but it can help parents feel more relaxed if you can establish some connections, e.g. that you both have a dog or that you like baking.

Packing a suitcase

At a conference many years ago, I met a Danish educator who explained how she helped children and parents make the transition into nursery school life using a toy suitcase. The suitcase symbolises the child starting a new journey.

At first the key person packs ten or so objects into the suitcase. Each object is chosen to represent something in the key person's life, e.g. a photograph of their own children, a postcard from a favourite place or a toy from their own childhood. The key person opens the suitcase and encourages the child to explore the objects and explains why each one is significant.

The child is then given their own empty suitcase which is taken home. The child, with the help of the parent, then selects items to bring into the setting to show the key person.

Once children have joined the setting, older children as part of circle time or in pairs, show each other the contents of their suitcases.

Where I have shared this tip and settings have used and adapted it, they have said that it has broken the ice with parents and that they have found it easier to talk to parents. Some settings have also used this as a transition tool to help children get to know their reception teacher on a visit.

Learning about the child

We also need to learn about the child from their parents, and tap into their parents' knowledge and expertise. The following questions or topics to talk about with parents can be helpful.

Reflection points

● What type of information do you currently collect from parents?

● Does the information provide you with an initial understanding of the child's temperament, interests and experiences?

Child's name _____

As a family we often use the name _____

(Names are very important markers of identity. As well as finding out the child's name it is also worth finding out if there are any nicknames at home and why they are used. You may also like to ask how the name was chosen for the child. In some languages children's names have particular meanings and even when they don't, most parents have a tale to tell about how the name was chosen.)

What is your child like? _____

_____

(How easily a child will settle will depend on many factors including their temperament. Finding out about how parents view their child is therefore useful and it may be worth explaining that if a child is naturally reserved, settling in may take a little longer.)

How does your child cope with separation? _____

_____

(Some children have already been looked after by family members, friends or other early years practitioners. It is worth finding out how that worked out, because if a child has had an 'unsuccessful' separation, there is a greater likelihood that they will take longer to settle in.)

What does your child like to play with and how do they interact with other children?

_____

_____

_____

(It is helpful to know what parents have noticed about how their child plays and what they enjoy doing. With parents who have two-year-olds, we may be able to reassure them that responses such as snatching or being very determined are perfectly normal.)

Learning about parents' feelings, expectations and ways of being with their child

As well as finding out about the child, it is also a good idea to find out about parents' expectations of their children and how they are feeling about leaving their child. It might be useful to look at the following questions:

- How do they feel about leaving their child with you?

- Is there anything that they are worried about?

- What would they most like their child to do next? (e.g. potty training)

- How do they comfort their child?

- What do they enjoy about their child?

- Is there anything that their child does that makes them cross?

- What are their hopes for their child in the future?

The process of settling in

For a number of years now, I have been advising settings to take a 'Settling in without tears' approach. Settings who have tried, and adapted it to their own situation, have reported that it has not only made a difference with children, but also to their relationships with parents. The aim of the child-led process is to build a bond between key person and child so that at the point the parents leave, the child is totally secure.

It is a five stage process which is carried out collaboratively with parents. How quickly children will move through the stages will depend on their age and temperament, the anxiety levels of their parents and their previous experience of being separated. It is based on a 'slide in/slide out' model whereby over the course of the stages, the key person increasingly interacts with the child whilst the parent increasingly 'slides out'. The final stage is where the child is happy to stay with their key person whilst their parents are not in the room.

Preparation

As this is a collaborative process, it is worth preparing an information sheet or explaining to parents each of the stages and their role within it. This is important because parents who are not sure what is about to happen can, through their body language, convey their anxiety to the child. It is also important to let parents know that their children are unlikely to be able to separate at the end of the first settling in visit as some familiarity with the setting is important. The exception to this is when children have siblings, pre-existing friendships or already know their key person.

In terms of preparation, it is helpful if you have already had a conversation with parents about their children's play interests and/or that you also have some interesting resources available.

The Five Stage Process

Stage 1

Learning to play with the key person

- Parent and child play together with the key person alongside

- Parent remains, but intermittently disengages from play

- This stage is completed when the key person and child can play together with the child making eye contact.

Stage 2

Learning that the key person is a safe person

Key person and child play together with parent alongside. Parent is not active in play and whilst physically there, is hardly making eye contact. (Parents may find it useful to look at a magazine.) On an agreed cue, parent wanders 2 metres or so away from the child and key person and then immediately returns. This is repeated several times.

Stage 3

Learning that parents may be out of sight but they always come back

- As Stage 2, but this time on an agreed cue the parent moves out of sight but still in the room (that might mean dodging behind a bookcase or popping into a storage cupboard!)

- The parent immediately returns

- This is repeated until the child is comfortable with the key person.

- This stage is completed when the child notices that the parent has moved, but is able to remain engaged with the key person.

Stage 4

Learning that the key person is there for you when your parent leaves

- The key person and child play together. The activity needs to be particularly engaging

- On an agreed cue, the parent announces that he/she needs to pop out to get something. They leave the room, but return back immediately. It is likely at first that the child will want to follow and if this is the case, the key person should walk with them and see if the child can be reassured. It is not a good idea to restrain the child

- It is essential that parents return immediately so that the child does not have time to become distressed

- This stage is likely to need repeating several times

- This stage is successfully completed when the parent is able to announce that they are popping out and the child is unfazed by this.

Stage 5

Practising separation

- As Stage 4, but gradually increase the time that the parent is out of the room

- This stage is successfully completed when the parent can be out of the room for 10 or 15 minutes and the child is relaxed in the presence of the key person

- Once this stage has been completed, then a decision can be made with the parents as to how long they should leave for. Ideally, it would be good to have a trial run of say, one hour, but not all parents will be in a position to do this.

Working with parents

This approach is meant to be collaborative. As well as focusing on the child, these settling in stages are also about parents getting to see that you can work well with their child. You may, for example ask their advice about what activities their child will enjoy doing and ask for their feedback about how they think your relationship with their child is developing.

Different ways of using this approach

Whilst the 'Settling in without tears' with its slide in/slide out approach needs to be retained, how it is organised in practice can vary according to the needs of parents and also the practicalities of your setting.

More than one child

It is possible to settle two children side by side, and in some ways this can work well because parents can support each other and are naturally likely to spend time focusing away from their children.

Session lengths and spacing

For some children and parents, it works well if they come for several short sessions over a number of weeks and work through the stages gradually. Childminders may arrange to meet parents at a playground or toddler group, for example. This little by little approach works well with the youngest children and also with children who have had a previous 'unsuccessful'

separation. It also works well if there is to be a long gap between the settling in process and actually starting off at the setting, e.g. summer holidays. This way the child will be more familiar with their key person and also the environment.

For parents who may be under pressure to get back to work, a different approach to session lengths and spacing will be needed. It may be better for children to come in on consecutive days at the start of the week, with the view to them starting, if they are ready, at the end of the week.

Stay and play

In some settings, parents are invited to stay and play, but during the session the key person and parent spend 15 minutes or so working intensively with the child.

Outdoors

In the summer, some settings do some of the early settling in stages outdoors, and do activities such as blowing bubbles or kicking a ball. Being outdoors can help children who have come to the setting before, but have not really settled in well. This can give them a fresh start.

Home visits

It is possible to do the first three stages as part of one or two home visits, although it is important that Stages 4 and 5 happen in the setting as children need to build up a goodbye routine there.

The impact of a poor settling in process

It is essential that everyone understands the long-term impact on children if settling is rushed and children are left before they are ready. Whilst sometimes parents are keen to leave their children, it is our task to dissuade them from doing so by pointing out that the short-term gain will be outweighed by potential long-term difficulties.

When children are not settled and secure, they are likely to show separation anxiety at the point of separation, which is damaging for the child but also very distressing for parents. Separation anxiety is characterised by 'protest' when children scream and howl and cannot be comforted. Once worn out, children may then become quiet and withdrawn. This phase is known as 'despair' although they may intermittently try to protest.

In the setting, we may only see the signs of separation anxiety, whilst at home and on the way to our setting, parents will be dealing with the fallout. This may include increased clinginess, disturbed sleep and regression. Parents will also report that it is an immense struggle to get their child ready to attend the session because the child will be uncooperative and may start the 'protest' phase as soon as they realise they are on the way to the setting. As separation anxiety persists and until such time as a child has developed a bond with an adult or another child

in the setting, this puts a huge pressure on the family regardless of any other difficulties that they may have.

There are longer-term effects too. Children whose experience of separation has been characterised by separation anxiety are more likely to find later transitions difficult. They often become the children who struggle when they have to change group or, later on in their school life, teachers.

Helping to create routines with parents

Once children are comfortable with the key person and they are ready to start off in the setting, it is worth discussing with parents how the routine of dropping them off and picking them up may work. Establishing a 'goodbye' routine is important because then it can become a template for the future. We are all different when it comes to saying goodbye and so helping parents to think about how they might like to approach it is useful. It is also worth looking at how you will be able to share information, comments and ideas together and generally keep in contact. If you have developed a good relationship at this point, you may find that talking about their child's development, next steps and possible activities comes quite naturally. This is another reason why taking time to settle children in alongside their parents can be so effective, as it establishes a way of working together.

Practical pressures on parents

Recognising that some families have significant pressures on them, such as domestic violence, low income, unemployment and housing issues, the key person also needs to be aware of some of the more common pressures that parents face.

It is often the smaller, more practical pressures that can be the 'last straw' for some families, and it is likely that at some time whilst children are with us, parents may ask for our advice or want signposting to other professionals. It is also worth remembering that when families are struggling with some of the more practical aspects of family life, they may not be in a position to focus on any of the well-meaning advice about sharing books, playing with their child more or contributing to a learning journal.

Sleep

No one is able to function without sleep. Very often the focus is on children having enough sleep, but it is also important to bear in mind that where sleep is an issue in a family, it may have a significant impact on the parents' ability to control their emotions, think strategically and manage their children's behaviour. Most of us find that we tend to be short-tempered and impatient when we are tired and this is not a good combination when faced with a toddler or young child who is also tired. Lack of sleep also means that parents may not have the energy or inclination to do those 'extra' valuable parenting activities such as sharing a book, playing a game or just chatting. Many parents put up with lack of sleep for too long and it is only when things reach crisis point that they feel that they can ask for help. As lack of sleep impacts on children's cognition as well as the emotional well-being of the family, it is important for us to pick up on this where it is a problem and encourage parents to seek help. This might be through a health visitor or even a referral to a sleep clinic.

Meal times

Most parents will have times when their children are picky or difficult eaters. For families on low incomes, food is a valuable commodity which they cannot afford to waste. This means that many families will choose food that they are sure that their children will eat rather than risk throwing anything away. This is sometimes an expensive and unhealthy option as children will often opt for ready meals and snacks that are low in nutrients, but high in fat. This is an area where, if parents feel that they can raise it with us, we can together develop strategies that will help children eat a wider range of foods.

There are many strategies and resources available that look at mealtimes and healthy eating. One that works well is a 'try before you buy' whereby children are introduced to foods in the setting and develop a taste for them so that parents know that if they buy them they will not be wasting their money. In terms of fussy eaters, there are many strategies that can be used and if necessary, parents may be interested in talking to a health visitor or gaining a referral to a dietician.

How well children sleep can make a difference to the emotional well-being of the family.

Parents often welcome tips about how to prevent challenging behaviour.

Battles between siblings

In early years settings, we often focus on individual children, but parents are often juggling the needs of two or more children. Battles between siblings are wearing for parents and can change the family dynamics, especially if it involves step or half-brothers and sisters. Instead of parents being able to spend positive time with their children, meal times, bedtimes and days out can feel like a contest. There are many reasons why it occurs, including sibling rivalry, tiredness, competition for parental affection as well as age differences and temperament. Sometimes, by discussing with parents what might be subconsciously motivating children to do 'battle' with each other, parents might be able to work out their next steps, e.g. if children are doing this to gain parental attention, it might be worth looking for more opportunities for each child to gain more attention or that children learn that when they cooperate they are rewarded with a family game or treat.

Managing behaviour

Whilst adults who work in early years settings have the advantage of having been trained in promoting positive behaviour, for many parents learning how to manage their children's behaviour is often trial and error, complicated by the emotions that parenthood brings. Attention-seeking behaviour, tantrums and being uncooperative are all common developmental behaviours that are not always easy to unpick.

Many parents will manage situations in similar ways to their own parents as this is their default setting. This may, in some cases, not always be effective – or even, these days, legal – as there are now tight laws restricting how children can be physically punished.

Behaviour is therefore one area that some parents may be interested in getting help with. This might be through providing resources such as magazine articles, having an information session – with parents making suggestions as to what should be covered – or clearly signposting parenting courses. Key persons may also model strategies or give tips, but they should always do so in ways that leave the parent feeling empowered rather than inadequate.

Reflection points

- What resources do you have available to help parents who need support over aspects of child-rearing?

- Do you have sufficient professional expertise to give accurate advice to parents?

- Have you a list of contacts to signpost parents to if they need additional help, e.g. health visitor?

Parent–child interactions are essential in promoting language development.

Supporting children's development at home

In addition to sharing information about their child's development through the use of photographs, video clips and discussions, some parents may also be interested to find out more about how they can help their child at home. If you work in an early years setting in England, you will need to demonstrate to Ofsted that you have successful strategies that encourage parents to support their child's development at home. The person best placed to talk to parents about their child's development is the key person, as they should have already established an effective working relationship with parents.

There are some specific areas of development that, when looked at with parents, can make a significant difference to their child's later achievement. These are:

- Communication and language
- Early literacy including early writing
- Early mathematics

Communication and language

One of the many ways that parents can make a tangible difference in their child's development is in the area of communication and language. This is because the bond that parents have allows them to tune into their children very accurately. They can tell, for example, when their toddler shakes their head, whether this is a definite 'no' or if there is room for some negotiation. In the same way, parents instinctively know whether or not their older child has understood something that another adult has said and if not, automatically rephrases at a level that their child can understand. As parents know what their child has experienced, they are also often able to make connections between what is happening and the child's past experience, e.g. 'that's the same as Granny's!' In addition, children usually want to communicate with their parents and enjoy their attention and so parents usually have a willing audience.

As communication and language underpins children's later academic and also social development, it is important that we celebrate the unique role that parents play. Interestingly, many parents do not realise that their 'chatter' has so much impact. They may not know that the walk to the corner shop or the brushing of hair in the morning is significant as an opportunity for children to acquire language skills, and that just by spending time talking and listening, they are giving their children the equivalent of language gold dust! Instead, I suspect that some parents assume that in early years settings, their children are getting all the interactions needed and so they may see their input as 'optional' rather than essential. They may not know that is hard for most practitioners in group care to provide three or four 10 minute conversations every day with their child. This is not a reflection on the quality of provision or the practitioner, but these are the practical limitations linked to adult–child ratios.

Optimum conditions for language

The great thing about communication and language between parent and child is that it can happen anywhere and anytime. The key thing is that the exchanges should be pleasurable to both adult and child. This may be when the parent joins in with their child's play, but not exclusively so. The reality is that not all parents find playing with their children easy or even enjoyable and a bored parent is less likely to communicate effectively.

Parents who are short of time may also find it hard to take time to stop what they need to do in order to play. The best interactions are always ones that are enjoyable, as both parents and children are likely to be responsive. This often allows the interactions to flow more easily and they may also last longer. Of course, parents need to be attentive to their child, but this does not mean that they cannot support their child's language as they involve their child in feeding the cat or preparing breakfast.

Everyday examples of when parents may be able to interact with their children include:

- Walking to and from the setting
- Going to get some shopping
- Bath/shower time
- Meal times
- Caring for plants/pets
- Preparing food
- Household chores, e.g. bringing in washing.

Reflection points

- How do you help parents realise the valuable role they have in supporting their child's development?

- How do you do this in ways that are not patronising?

- How do you ensure that any suggestions are realistic and achievable for parents?

Early literacy including early writing

There is some research to show that where parents are involved in early literacy activities, there is a significant impact on children's later attitudes as well as skills.

Modelling how to share a book with child and parent

Whilst for some parents it feels natural to share books with their children, this is not the case for all parents. There are many ways in which we can help parents enjoy sharing books with their children, although we should always be mindful that some parents' own literacy levels may be a barrier. For some parents, offering to show them how you share a book with their child might be helpful. Parents may not necessarily know how to maintain children's attention in a book or the importance of spending time talking about what is in the pictures. Tips such as what to do if their child wants to turn the pages backwards or if the child becomes restless can give parents confidence. Afterwards, you could offer to lend the book to the parent. Some settings have spaces where parents and their children can look at books together. These books can also be lent to parents if they wish.

Choosing successful books

It is always helpful for parents who are not used to sharing a book with their child, to be lent or given a book that is pretty much guaranteed to be a success. We can help to do this by finding a book that is simple to read, but which the child is interested in, and then sharing it a few times with the child first. This way the child will already be familiar with it when the parent looks at it.

Local libraries

Many parents are not aware that their local library will let them borrow many books for free. Some settings ask permission from parents to get a library card for their children or arrange to meet them in the library. One of the concerns from many parents is what will happen if the books get damaged or lost. Fortunately, most libraries have a fairly relaxed policy on this.

Making and using 'story sacks'

A story sack is a picture book with accompanying props. Many settings have had success with these by involving parents in making them, but also by lending them out. Suggestion cards to help parents know how to use them are a good idea as they can act as prompts for parents who are unsure.

Sharing a book with a parent can give children an early interest in reading.

Parent-to-parent recommendations

Peer to peer support is known to be a useful and supportive mechanism. Some settings have, using social media, encouraged parents to recommend books to others that they and their child have enjoyed together or conversely ones to avoid!

Early writing

One of the easiest ways for parents to support their child's early writing is to simply put out some markers, crayons and pencils and some paper on a table and show interest in what their child is doing. It is also helpful if parents know a little about the stages of writing and the importance of the mark making phase as well as the development of the pencil grip (see Chapter 8, page 147). As some parents may not be confident writers themselves, it is important to be sensitive to this and also to reassure them that their child will just gain from their being interested in their early mark making and writing. Where parents feel able to write in front of their child, particularly dads in front of their sons, this can be a very powerful motivator for children.

Parents may also like to get involved in helping their children learn specific handwriting movements, e.g. making rotational marks on the door of the shower with a sponge or making a letter shape with a duster on a table!

Reflection points

- How do you provide information to parents about their role in supporting literacy at home?

- Do you share resources and ideas with them?

- How do you empower parents to feel that their input matters?

Early mathematics

As with literacy, some parents may not feel that they are good at maths. The good news to get across to parents is that the type of activities that can help their children are very easy to do. They include: counting, matching and sorting. Ideally, the key person will know the parents well enough to be able to give examples of how these activities can be slotted into everyday life, e.g. if parents have to walk up a few steps to the entrance of their home, this might be an opportunity to count or if they have three pets that need feeding, this might be another counting opportunity.

There are other activities that parents might be interested in carrying out, such as jigsaw puzzles or simple games, and it is always worth having a collection of age-/stage-appropriate resources that parents can borrow. As some people learn through watching, it can be helpful to offer to show parents how you use these resources with their children.

Summary

We have seen that the issues that surround parenting are complex. No two parents are the same, and so the level of information and support that they need may be very different. We have also seen the multiple factors that may affect parents' ability to engage with us. This means that there can never be a set formula as to how best to work with parents, Instead, we constantly need to reflect on our approach and whether it is effective in supporting parents and building a strong working relationship, the foundations of which I believe lie in having an effective settling in process.

Chapter 2

Creating a rich play environment

Play is central to a fulfilling childhood and it must not be edged out just because children don't always have the resources, physical space or opportunities to play freely in their own homes. To close the gap and reduce educational disadvantage, we need to think carefully about the play environments that we provide and the role of the adult within them.

Although in the next chapter I discuss education programmes for children that are likely to be adult-initiated to begin with, it is important that we first consider the importance of creating rich play environments. Therefore, in this chapter we look at the importance of a rich play environment and ways in which we can plan, create and assess such an environment.

Play should be a significant part of every childhood.

The importance of a rich play environment

Much has been written about the benefits of play over the years. For children who are at risk of educational disadvantage, a rich play environment can support them in variety of ways.

Well-being and freedom

Whilst some children are 'lucky' and are in family structures that offer security and stability, other children are not as fortunate. Play can offer a route for children to develop a sense of well-being and freedom in a safe environment. For some children, play offers an escape route from anxiety and stress. This may lead to children who need opportunities to engage in some repetition of movements such as pouring water over and over again. For other children, there may be a need to gain control over materials or possibly show quite destructive behaviours. They may, for example, want to pound dough aggressively or squash sandcastles down with a toy car.

Sensory exploration

'Lucky' children often have a range of materials and toys to play with and places to explore. This may include slopes to run down, balls to catch and bushes to hide in. This rich tapestry gives children plenty of first-hand knowledge of sensory experiences that are very stimulating. Ideally, in creating an exciting play environment, we need to think about how we might replicate some of these experiences.

Self-regulation

Self-regulation seems to play an important part in children's later success. Through play, children can practise and develop some key aspects of self-regulation. In play, for example, children often set their own challenges. This can be anything from wanting to dig a tunnel in the mud through to laying out a line of toy cars. By focusing their attention and also persevering in a task, children can learn to delay gratification until the task has been finished. Play with other children also supports other key features of self-regulatory behaviour such as waiting for a turn and not always being able to lead or win a game.

Physical activity

All children need high levels of physical activity to remain healthy. The current recommendation for children under five years is 3 hours a day. Play is a key way in which this level of physical activity can be undertaken without the need for any formal exercise. Through play, children can also develop both fine and gross motor skills as well as all round co-ordination skills in a safe environment. This last point is important because some children are developing these skills at home, but in more hazardous conditions.

Children need three hours a day of physical activity.

Exploration of roles

From around two and half or so, children usually start to explore roles. These may be in terms of their gender, their place in the family or other roles that they have seen either at first hand by observing adults or at second hand via screens by watching films, computer games or television programmes. For some children, the roles they have seen adults play on and off screen may be disturbing, violent or threatening. Play offers children a safe opportunity to explore and understand what they have seen and find a pathway through it. When it comes to gender, a rich play environment can, in part, challenge and rebalance the gender roles.

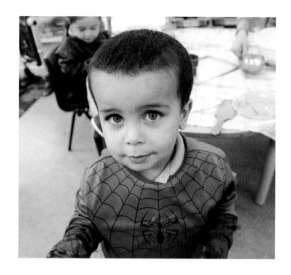

Issues to consider when creating a rich play environment

There are some key issues that you may wish to reflect on when creating a rich play environment that will support children who are at risk of disadvantage. By reflecting on these in the context of the children that you work with, you are more likely to create an environment that will support their needs.

Experience of play

When creating a rich play environment, you may need to think about children's previous experience of play. Although many children have had plenty of opportunities to play and know how to play with and treat resources, for other children this may not be the case. For some children, a large space and a wide choice of resources may actually be overwhelming for them and a barrier to their participation in play. You might consider whether children need additional mentoring as to how to play, including more direction as to what to do with specific resources.

Balance of child-initiated play

There is no official guidance about the amount of time that children should spend in child-initiated activities, and so this is one of the decisions that individual settings need to make. Having said that, the EPPE project reported that in high quality pre-school provision, adults were very involved in initiating play and activities. When it comes to your setting, it is always worth thinking about what the children that you work with will need. This will include how much adult input they are getting from their home environment and whether individual children have specific developmental needs and how these are best met.

Directing children towards a range of play types

We know that each type of play, such as physical play or construction, offers different developmental benefits. One of the issues that we might like to think about is whether there are times when children should be encouraged to play with materials that they do not normally choose to play with. This goes back to a long-standing debate within the early years about how much adult-led activity should be on offer in your setting.

Designing an environment for play

There is no 'ideal' way of setting out and resourcing an environment for any given group of children. The reality is that every setting is different, and even when something is working it may not be as effective for a different cohort or combination of children. In addition, as children develop, their needs change and so it is best to think of the play environment as one that evolves around the developing and changing needs and interests of the children.

Having said that, there are some factors that I believe need to be carefully considered if the play environment is going to be genuinely enriching for those children whose development may otherwise be compromised.

Staffing

My current starting point when working with settings is to start by recognising the potential impact of the adult-child ratio that is available. This is because it links to the practicalities of what can be put out, how space can be managed and the amount of time available to set up and maintain a play environment.

In well-staffed environments where adult–child ratios exceed the minimum regulatory limits, providing a rich and safe play environment is fairly straightforward. On the other hand, in

Learning through child-initiated play can be enhanced by adults.

settings that only staff to the minimum, especially maintained schools where a 1:13 ratio is used, this is much more of a challenge and while you should always begin by petitioning for better ratios, it may be that you will need to be strategic in your layout and resources.

Possibilities for sustained language

A rich play environment that will make a difference to children's lives needs to facilitate sustained adult-child interactions. The EPPE project reported that high quality pre-school provisions were characterised not only by a balance between adult-led and child-initiated activity, but also that during child-initiated activity, adults were providing high-quality interactions.

Again, this goes back to staffing, as there needs to be sufficient members of staff to be able to spend time interacting with children. Even with sufficient staff, where significant numbers of children have language needs, it will be important to create a play environment that prioritises the development of language.

Background noise

Another good starting point for your planning is to think about levels of background noise. This is particularly important when working with the under threes who are less likely to talk when there is a lot of ambient noise. There are many strategies to reduce background noise. Interestingly, when they are employed, they also impact on children's play and use of space.

Cosy corners, tents and dens
This can be done using cushions, pop-up tents, fabrics and commercially-bought structures, e.g. domes and pagodas.

Creating defined areas within large rooms
By putting furniture such as bookcases adjacent to walls, sound can be deflected. The smaller spaces created also help children to communicate with each other without needing to raise their voices.

Using sound-absorbing materials
Carpets, rugs and soundproofing foam can be used to cut ambient noise. The latter is particularly helpful in large rooms.

Resources and equipment

It is important to audit your resources and equipment and think about how they contribute to the quality of adult-child interaction. Ideally, you want as many activities and resources that encourage children to communicate with each other or with adults as much as possible. This is the 'win-win' situation for a rich play environment, as children are not only enjoying their play, but their language development is also being supported.

To ensure that children's language is being maximised, it is important that every area of your environment is viewed objectively in terms of how it facilitates interaction. When settings audit their provision for this, they can find some surprises.

Some settings find that climbing frames and slides which require an adult to be on 'standby', do not actually facilitate high levels of quality interaction. Instead, adults may only be using 'functional language' and where there are conversations between child and adult, they may be quite perfunctory with the adult finding it hard to make eye contact whilst they supervise the other children. Although children may be happy using such equipment, I would argue that they may not be developing any or many new skills. On the other hand, where settings put out car tyres, wooden planks and crates, language interactions can be stronger as it is easier for the adult and other children to become involved in play. This more open-ended play not only delivers on developing children's balance and co-ordination, but it can be very empowering for children. Since items of play equipment are lower and there is less risk of an accident, children also play independently.

Layout

Some layouts seem to allow for more interaction than others. It is worth watching the 'flow' of children using a provision because some layouts seem to encourage children to merely 'flit' from one activity to another. Although a degree of this is inevitable as young children are easily distracted, it is important to monitor it, as 'flitting' can impact on both children's learning and levels of interaction. Where settings create smaller cosy spaces, the 'flit' factor seems to recede, although of course it depends on whether what is in the small cosy spaces is of interest to the children.

Reflection points

- Which areas seem to generate the best child-child interactions and adult-child interactions?

- Where are adults best able to 'stay and play' with children?

- Are there are any areas where adults' language tends to be simply 'functional', e.g. 'Wait a minute', 'Careful!' or 'Don't run!'?

- What are the background noise levels in different areas of the provision and at different times?

Open-ended resources are important for quality play and interactions.

Recognising children's stage of play

An important factor in resourcing and setting up the play environment is the stage of children's play. Play and development levels are linked, which means that a four-year-old with the language level of a two-year-old is more likely to play in ways that are normally associated with the younger age. Language in particular seems to have an impact on children's play, with children who are talking confidently usually engaging well with role play, small world play and co-operative ventures with other children.

By and large, for younger children whose language is still very much in development, their play is often sensory or governed by gross motor movements.

The play of a child whose language is fairly fluent tends to veer more towards role play and play that involves others. On the other hand, a four-year-old with limited language may find it hard to engage with role play type activities or those requiring language. Bringing the different experiences and developmental needs of children together to create an 'ideal' play environment is not easy, but this is perhaps one of the most exciting challenges for us to fully consider.

Reflection points

- How do audit your play provision to ensure that it meets children's stage of play?

- When children are with you for a number of years, how do you ensure that your play provision continues to excite and provide challenge?

Finding the balance between a high-maintenance and a sterile environment

Everyone's view about how to organise a play environment may be different, although the key consideration must be meeting children's needs and ensuring that there is plenty of challenge, creativity and enjoyment.

One of the factors that needs plenty of thought is how to create an environment that can be maintained by both children and adults. This is an essential discussion for several reasons. Firstly, some children need to experience an orderly environment for their own well-being and self-regulation because their home environments are chaotic. They also need to experience how to create order for themselves. By being physically involved in restoring order can be a useful starting point. Secondly, where adult interactions are a priority in order to support children's language level, an environment that is high-maintenance means that precious adult time is spent tidying up rather than engaging with children. In addition, where play environments become degraded because children and adults cannot maintain them, children can quickly lose the means and the focus to genuinely benefit from the play opportunities. This in turn can affect their behaviour, especially for children who have low levels of self-regulation.

I hasten to add that I am not advocating sterile environments that are over-structured, as children do need opportunities to explore and be creative. There is also no one-size-fits-all approach here, but it is important that we are objective about how well the play environment is working for the children and whether the play environment supports adult–child interactions. On page 41, we look at an observation method that can help adults to evaluate their play environment and how well it supports children's enjoyment and engagement.

Less is more

To maintain play environments it can be helpful to use the 'less is more' principle. The idea behind this is to consider how many of any one particular resource will actually be needed to support play. In my experience, it is not the duplication of materials that enhances children's play, but the combinations of materials that do this. 'Less is more' is not about cutting down the number of play opportunities for children.

'Less is more' is achieved by observing children's habits and looking at which items they choose and how they play with them. It also means thinking about how many children at any one time need the resource. A good example of this is the large crate of toy cars that many settings put out. This resource usually appeals to four or five children at any one time, but the crate often contains far more cars than are actually needed. Children just tip them out onto the floor to find their 'favourites' and discard the rest, but they still end up getting in the way of the play. The large quantity of unwanted cars also tends to be overwhelming when it comes to tidying up, so this job often falls to the adult.

The 'less is more' approach would result in reorganising the cars to reflect children's favourites so that children can easily find the cars they want. It would also mean sifting through the remaining cars and putting them into smaller groups that children could access if they needed more cars at some point. As the 'less is more' principle is also about variety, thought would also be given to providing complementary resources for this play, e.g. a tub of cardboard tubes to act as tunnels and a container of cardboard strips to act as roads.

Ideally, the sorting and repackaging of materials is done with children so that they take some ownership of the resources and their presentation.

Things to consider when taking a 'less is more' approach:

- How many children usually play with this resource at any one time?

- How many items do they actually need?

- Which are the favourites?

- Is there sufficient variety?

- How easy will it be for children to tidy up or restore the environment when they have finished?

Players or doers?

Another factor in setting up and resourcing a play environment is the adults. As adults, we all have individual strengths and weaknesses as well as preferences as to what we enjoy doing with children. Where adults are working as part of a team, it is worth reflecting on adults' strengths and play preferences. This is because when adults are genuinely enjoying their play with children, they are more likely to interact and extend children's play. Children are also likely to respond better as they can sense whether we are good play companions or not.

Some adults are great at playing in the role play area with children (the players), others come into their own when they are cooking with children or joining in games such as snap (the doers!). Some adults have no particular preference and enjoy both styles of working with children. Many childminders fit into this category, and of course we should all be able to turn our hand to both styles when needed! Having said this, understanding your strengths and those of the adults around you can make for better adult-child interaction.

Reflection points

- If you work in a team, have you considered your own play preferences?

- Are there any play types that you find harder to support?

Some adults are naturally good play companions for children.

Assessing the play environment

It is worth observing and reviewing your play provision from time to time, watching how children are using it and also how much interaction it is generating. It is also helpful to understand the reasons why individual children find it hard to engage with play. For a while now, I have combined two classic observation methods in order to observe groups of children at play. Though this is not the only way to observe children at play, settings that have tried it report that it has helped them to understand more about the play environment and also about the adults' role within it.

Using the observation method

The group recording sheet is a simple time sample method combined with a coding system adapted from the target child method. You can observe the play of up to ten children using this method. Each child should be observed during five minute intervals. It is not a detailed observation, but will give you an overview as to where children are, what they are doing and whether or not they are interacting with other children or adults. This observation method will often provide a starting point for other more detailed observations of individual children.

Starting out

Begin by deciding at what time would be best to observe the environment in action. It may be that you want to observe how quickly children settle into play when they first arrive or that you want to investigate why at certain times children seem to be less engaged. Next consider whether there are any particular children that you wish to follow, this may include children who need high levels of interaction.

Creating the observation sheet

Because I am combining a time sample with a target child method, I construct a simple grid (see opposite page). The far left column is for timings. I normally observe in five-minute slots. The other columns record children's individual activity. I normally begin by observing three or so children and assuming that they are quite settled, I then add other children to my sheet. At first, I just note their location and whether or not they are with other adults or children. At the start of every five-minute slot, I record whether they are still involved in the activity. During each of the five-minute slots, I will keep glancing between children to see whether they have moved on or whether there are tangible differences in either how they are playing or who they are with. Once I feel that I have a measure of their activity, I also focus on how engaged they are. This I note on a 1–5 engagement score. As much recording as possible is carried out using codes or abbreviations. You can use the classic codes of the target child or you can, as I have, develop your own over time. Afterwards, I write down any additional information that I have noted but not yet recorded.

These children are highly engaged and so can benefit from this play environment.

Observation sheet

Time	Amy	Josie	Kyle	Baran	Michael	Sam
10.00	Sand ←→ Sand ↓	Sand ↓	Cars © → Train → Cars ↓	~~~→ ~~~→	Paints Ⓐ ⑤ ↓	Water Pouring ↓
10.05	↓ ←→↓ Hiding hands Laughing ↓		Using tubes © Building roads ↓	Sand → Ⓐ ~~~→	Ⓐ Mixes colours ↓	Collects bottles ↓ C
10.10	↓ ←→↓ Hiding objects Turn taking ✓✓ ⑤ ↓		©	Dough ② Low engagement ↓	Explores sponges Ⓐ ↓	Pouring bottle to bottle ↓ C ⑤
10.15	↓ Sand ② ~~~→	→ Role play C	©	~~~→ Cars Watches Kyle + Ed ~~~→	→ Wash hands No more paper!	Bottles and buckets C ↓
10.20	Dough → Role play ↓	'Shop Keeper' © ↓	→ Ⓐ © Shows adult ↓	~~~→ Outdoors trike ④	Dough Rolls + cuts © 'snakes' ↓	No responses to other child pouring! C ↓
10.25	↓ Customer ←→→↓	Shop keeper © ↓	Complex ↓ road © system ↓	Trike ↓	Making © ⑤ snakes race ↓	Bottles pouring ↓ C
10.30	↓ C Collects other objects ③	↓ C Shop keeper counts money	High ↓ engagement ↓ ⑤ ©	↓ Kicks ball Ⓐ ~~~→	Ⓐ © Counting → snack ↓	↓ A C
10.35	Buying ←→ Selling + advice!! → Snack ←→ Snack		Adds farm animals	~~~→ Indoors	↓ Snack	→ Aprons → Toilet

Code

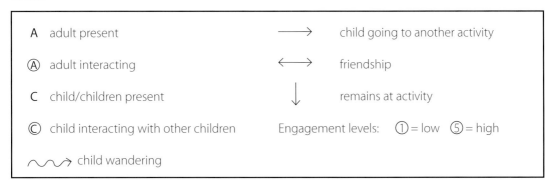

A   adult present   ⟶   child going to another activity

Ⓐ   adult interacting   ⟷   friendship

C   child/children present   ↓   remains at activity

©   child interacting with other children   Engagement levels: ① = low   ⑤ = high

~~~→   child wandering

Length and focus of observation

I tend to record for at least 40 minutes, preferably an hour. Therefore, if you are offering three-hour sessions, this will be a third of the children's time with you. I also try and sample the activity of at least eight children. If you find it hard to do, this mainly because children tend to keep flitting from one activity to another, this is already telling you quite a lot about the effectiveness of your provision. Although you will need to consider your own focus for any observation, these are the questions that I am particularly concerned with:

- How long do children stay with an activity they have chosen themselves?

- To what extent are they fully engaged in their activity?

- Do they interact with other children?

- Do they interact with any adults? If so, for how long and who initiates this?

- Why do children leave their chosen activities? For example, is it because a friend left or to seek out an adult?

- Are there any children who find it hard to settle to any activity? If so, do adults seem to notice this?

- Are there any areas of the play environment that seem to be less of interest?

Reflecting on the observation

By observing your play environment and how children use it, you should gain plenty of information that you can use as a starting point for development or for reflection. Although this type of observation does not drill down into individual children's development, you may find that something about the way a child interacts, plays or concentrates will attract your attention. This then becomes a starting point for individual targeted observations about the child.

Do you have a long term plan for your role play area?

Coloured modelling clay has been put out to give these children a new experience of a malleable material.

Creating a long-term plan for play opportunities

One of the key challenges when providing a rich play environment is to think about how it can continue to meet children's changing play needs. This should to be a particular focus if you are working with children who are likely to be in the same space for more than a year or so. The child at age two who is fascinated by making the water wheel turn around, may not pay more than a passing regard for it two years later when they have clocked up over a thousand hours in your setting. Children can be hungry consumers when it comes to play and this is of course links back to the strides that they are making in all aspects of their development.

With every new play opportunity that captures a child's interest, there are immediate possibilities for the learning of new skills and concepts. As part of long-term planning, you should think about how you can keep changing your play environment and thus maintain interest. Of course, it will always be important to retain equipment and materials that are 'bestsellers'

or that individual children are interested in, but there is also a place for rotation and innovation. The chart on the next page gives some examples of how you might reflect on your long-term provision to ensure that children's interest and satisfaction in some of the key play types can be maintained, but also that opportunities for learning are challenging.

Key play types

Role play	Very effective in helping children develop vocabulary and social skills and provides possibilities for early literacy and numeracy.	• Do you have a long-term plan for role play topics in your setting? • Are props sufficiently detailed to provide children with opportunities to learn specific vocabulary and for early mathematics, e.g. a shoe gauge for use in your shoe shop; coat hangers with sizes on them…?
Malleable materials	Very effective in developing fine manipulative skills as well as links to imaginative play and role play. Supports children's creativity and emotional well-being.	• Do you have a long-term plan to introduce different types of malleable materials for children to explore? • Do you provide a range of detailed props that will allow children to combine this with role play, e.g. chef's aprons, pastry brush…? • Do you provide contrasting malleable materials so that children can explore differences in texture and form? • Do you have a long-term plan so that over time children are able to make their own dough independently? • Do you provide early literacy and mathematical props alongside malleable materials, e.g. birthday cards, menus, order sheets…?
Water and sand	Very effective at supporting children's emotional well-being as well as fine manipulative skills. Can provide a stimulus for early maths and early science if carefully resourced and supported with sensitive adult input.	• Do you have a long-term plan so that children explore different depths and measures of sand and water? • Do you provide increasingly challenging resources that will encourage children to accurately explore measuring? • Do you provide props that will support children's mathematical skills, e.g. ice cube trays, measuring jugs, numbers…? • Are adults able to give accurate explanations to scientific concepts, e.g. why items may float on top of the water, whilst others sink?
Construction play	Very effective in developing spatial awareness, problem-solving and early science. (See Chapter 9, page 156)	• How do you ensure that all children access construction play regularly? • Do you have a long-term plan to support children's progress using different types of construction toys e.g. duplo or lego? • Do adults support children?
Mark-making (See Chapter 8, page 141), painting and collage	Effective in encouraging early writing and fine manipulative movements. Supports children's creativity and interest in design.	• Do you have a long-term plan to support children's progress in using a range of mark-making tools, e.g. from palm-held markers to pencils? • Do you have a long-term plan to support children's progress in exploring paint and painting techniques, e.g. pallettes, shades of colours, brushes, sponges, rollers…? • Do you have short-term plans to rotate and combine materials to ensure challenge and interest? • How do you ensure that all children are able to engage in and access this type of play?

As well as relying on the traditional toys and resources that most early years settings have, we also need to make sure that the play environment contains a few surprises or possibilities for children. This is particularly important for children who spend many hours with us or in similar settings. The phrase 'rich, varied and imaginative' comes from the 2015 Ofsted evaluation schedule and reminds us that play and learning should be creative and the very opposite of boring.

Language provocations

A useful way of creating a rich, varied and imaginative environment is to look at planning language provocations. These are small adjustments or surprises in the environment that will provoke interest and discussion. This could be as simple as an adult wearing a crown or unusual headwear through to a suitcase filled with clothes put in the outdoor area.

Loose part play

As children's development progresses, they will also need increasing opportunities to combine materials and objects as part of their play. One way of keeping the play environment dynamic is to create opportunities for children to 'find' interesting objects. These are put out randomly in the play environment, e.g. a long strip of fabric, a 10 litre bucket, a cardboard tube and a rubber plunger. Children can then choose whether to ignore, use or combine these objects. This is sometimes referred to as 'loose part play'. In some ways it could be seen as an extension of treasure basket or heuristic play as it allows children to explore and use objects in an open-ended way.

Summary

In this chapter, we have seen that play plays an important role in children's development. We have also seen that there are issues that we need to explore when thinking about how we might support children who are at risk of disadvantage. They include the extent to which we might need to coach children as they play and how we create a play provision that will develop children's language and also that will remain challenging for them.

Chapter 3

Constructing an education programme

Closing the gap in attainment relies on every setting thinking about the experiences and opportunities that will help all children make rapid progress in their development.

Whilst all early years settings have an early years curriculum to follow, the curriculum does not go into any depth about what you actually need to do on a day-to-day basis, week by week. This means that a child in one setting will have a very different experience from a child in another. In many ways this is rather wonderful as it means that we can have a diversity of approaches. It does, however, mean that settings have to establish their own navigation systems in terms of their practice. This is straightforward for settings that are founded on pedagogical beliefs and have clear principles about childhood and child development that guide their work. If you are not in such a setting, you will need to make active choices about the journey that children will take when they are with you. In the case of children who are at risk of disadvantage, planning strategically for their journey is critical.

In this chapter, I want to explore the importance of developing a long-term and strategic approach to supporting children who are at risk of disadvantage.

This setting has decided to focus on books as an essential part of their education programme.

The importance of planning for the long term

'Lucky' children often have 'safety nets' in the form of parents' resources, knowledge and contacts, which support their development. They may also have access to a range of experiences that will enrich their development and support their confidence.

I would therefore argue that we need to create our own safety nets to support children who are at risk of disadvantage, to ensure that they have some of the same experiences and opportunities. Whilst part of the safety net is around creating supportive relationships with them (See chapter 5, page 68), the other aspect of the safety net is to provide them with a range of opportunities that will support their development, especially in key areas such as communication and language.

The idea of an 'education programme' or whatever term you choose to use, is to create a long-term plan which acts as a clear road map for children's journeys while they are in your care. It picks up on what you know about the children in your area and their needs. It may mean, for example, that you decide that when children leave your setting, they will have had opportunities to play with a range of malleable materials including stretchy dough and cooked dough, but also clay, silly putty and plasticine. It may also mean that children, if stage appropriate, have experienced traditional games such as picture lotto, snap and dominoes. They may also have posted a letter, grown a vegetable and been to a local museum. Although such opportunities may arise through day-to-day or even week by week planning, this is likely to be a more random approach and so opportunities to enhance children's experiences and play may sometimes be missed. Having a long-term plan provides a strategic tool that allows you to put in place the skills, opportunities and experiences that you have identified as important for the children that you work with.

Is planning exclusively for children's interests in their overall best interest?

Some settings take the line that they exclusively plan and develop activities based on children's current interests. Children's interests are of course important and must be incorporated into short-term planning, but we also have to be thoughtful about the potential limitations of this approach. Here are a few of questions that you might like to reflect on, which may trigger some interesting discussions in your work with others.

Can children make genuine choices if they have limited experiences?

Some children have not had many opportunities to experience a wide range of opportunities outside of the setting. This means that they are limited to what they can show an interest in. Put simply, a child cannot choose to play or ask for an activity that they do not know exists! A child who does not know about farms may not ask to play with a farm set or show interest in picking up a book about farms. In the same way, a child who has not experienced cooking may not ask to cook. By having a plan to introduce new play opportunities, a range of experiences and some adult-led activities, the possibilities for children increase which will eventually mean that they can have genuine interests and preferences.

Is there a danger of children restricting their learning as they may choose 'gendered' activities?

We live in an increasingly gendered age in terms of early childhood. This can mean that some children from around three onwards will restrict what they choose to play with according to their developing concept of gender. By only planning according to children's interests, there is a danger that children may not be using the full range of play types and this in turn may limit their development. Construction play, for example, is particularly good at helping children to develop spatial awareness, sequencing and planning skills and if there is a group of children who regularly does not use this play type, these skills may not be developed.

How can you be sure that children have the breadth of learning opportunities and skills?

Although in theory it is possible to encompass early mark making, jigsaws and sharing books into children's interests, the reality is that unless there are very good adult–child ratios and a child who is open to suggestion, this is quite hard to do. If we look at 'lucky' children, we will see that they do not spend all of their time only doing what they feel like doing. Instead, adults will at times take the lead, e.g. taking them to the park or asking the child to help them feed the cat. At these times a line of 'no refusal' is in place because parents recognise that overall it is for their children's benefit.

The wider issues in creating an education programme

There is no single formula for how to create an education programme that will act as a safety net for disadvantaged children. Every setting needs to develop its own pathway. In doing this, a good starting point is to consider some of the wider issues that will underpin your approach.

The nature of childhood

On average children are now spending longer than ever in early years settings. A child who currently begins their funded hours at two-years-old and leaves aged four years, six months will have clocked up 1,450 hours in a setting. This represents a significant part of their early childhood and so we do need to think about the memories and experiences that we leave them with. In some ways this touches at the heart of what we think a golden childhood should look like. If you are working with other adults, this is an important discussion to have and you may like to consider some of the following questions:

- What is the role of play within childhood?

- How important are outdoor experiences for childhood?

- How do adults figure in childhood and what should their role be?

- What resources or opportunities are important in childhood?

- What would 'lucky' children be doing in this time if they were at home with supportive parents?

Knowledge of child development and latest research

For an education programme to be effective, it has to be based on a good working knowledge of child development. As theories of child development are constantly evolving in line with research, it is worth taking time to revisit what you know and update your knowledge. It is also worth looking at research that has focused on effective practice in supporting children who are at risk of disadvantage and then considering the key messages in terms of your own practice. In particular, you could look at the findings of the EPPE project (see Introduction, page 9) as well as research reports from organisations such as the Sutton Trust (www.suttontrust.com).

Reflection points

- Do you regularly read articles or books about early years education?

- Have you read any reports about supporting children at risk of disadvantage?

This setting has a focus on outdoor play. Is this a major focus for your setting?

Exploring alternative ways of working

To get a sense of how your approach might work, it is worth visiting other early years settings both in your local area and, if possible, in other regions. If you are part of an association such as PACEY, PLA or NDNA, it should be possible to make contact with your head office and ask them for a contact in another area. You may also find it helpful to visit settings that are based on a clear philosophy or pedagogy such as Montessori, Froebel, HighScope or Reggio Emilia. Visiting other settings is always interesting. You are likely to find things to make you reflect, or see ideas that you can think about incorporating into your practice. It is also good to find other interested professionals with whom you can have a discussion.

Reflection points

- What settings are there in your local area that you could visit?

- Have you visited a setting that takes a different approach to yours?

Using developmental norms to inform a programme

It can be helpful to consult a range of materials that look at developmental norms such as those used by health professionals including speech and language therapists (see Bibliography and further reading, page 183) to help create an education programme. These are often more specific, detailed and sequential than the outcomes within some early years curricula. They are also based on research that has studied wide groups of children's development rather than a politician's 'wishlist'. The advantage of using them is that you will be able to work out what the typical direction of travel is likely to be across the key classical areas of child development. You may use this to help you plan self-care activities across the time that children are with you, for example, if you know that most children at three, are still using a spoon and fork, but will be starting to use a knife at four. (Mary Sheridan, *From Birth to Five Years*)

Where settings have a good understanding of developmental norms, it helps them to plan age-/stage-appropriate resources and activities. They know, for example, that children at two are unlikely to be ready for scissors, but will be able to enjoy collage materials. They also know that children under eighteen months will routinely take objects to their mouths to explore and so this informs the resources that are chosen. It also helps them to see how the acquisition of skills such as learning to catch a ball or use a tripod grasp can be broken down into developmental steps.

Using developmental norms to support precise assessment

Settings working with children at risk of disadvantage need to have an accurate picture of how these children are faring in relation to their 'lucky' peers. This is important because without a clear reference, we often base our expectations of children's development on the cohort we are working with. Thus in a setting where many children have some level of language delay, the child who is showing typical development, may be seen as 'exceeding' the norms and leading to an underestimation of the needs of the other children. (If you are working in an early years setting in England, it is worth being aware that Ofsted are expecting precise assessment and also that you are able to reflect on children's progress in relation to the expected development of others.) Using developmental norms can also be helpful when tailoring plans and activities for individual children. By recognising that a child needs additional support and the extent of this need, settings can then adapt their plans more effectively for individual children. This might include providing more input, but also breaking down skill acquisition into smaller steps.

Reflection points

- How do you ensure that children have opportunities to acquire age- or stage-appropriate skills?

- How do you ensure that children's level of skill is increasing in line with age/stage normative development?

- How do you ensure that children who need additional input or interventions are accurately identified?

Precise assessment of children's skills and knowledge is essential.

Tailoring the education programme to your setting

Although there may be larger issues to consider about the direction of your setting, it is also important to tailor your education programme to the actual needs of your children. This will depend on quite a few factors.

Attendance

The age at which children typically start in your setting and how long they spend with you will influence your provision. In some settings, children start at two-years-old and so will spend two or even close to three years in a setting. This means that when building a programme, you will need to think about how their play and experiences will develop with them. Settings that do not focus on this, often report that children in the final weeks have 'outgrown' the setting and are ready to move on.

This play is challenging for this two-year-old, but will it remain so when this child is four?

In addition to the starting age, the length of sessions also has an impact on how you might plan a programme. Three-hour sessions are very different in nature to all-day provision. Many sessional providers find that time flies by as it takes some children a little while to reconnect with their key person and also the routines of the setting.

Reflection points

- What is the total amount of time that children will spend in your setting?

- How do you ensure that the play and experiences on offer maintain their learning challenge?

- When children are with you for a limited time, how do you balance the session to ensure that it maximises their learning?

Auditing the needs of the children

No education programme will be effective without tuning in to the needs of the children that you work with. You will need to reflect on the profiles of children coming in to your setting so that you can tailor your approach. It is particularly helpful to look for recurring trends. Many early years settings say in answer to this that their children are particularly in need of communication and language skills and skills related to self-regulation. (If you work in early years settings in England, Ofsted will pick up on whether you are aware of development across groups of children.) In addition, if there are one or two schools in your area that most children go to, it might be worth talking to them about their data as children progress through the school. Their insights might again inform your decision-making about how best to build the foundations on which children can later thrive.

Reflection points

- From your own assessment of groups of children in your setting, what do you feel are the key areas in which children need additional support?

- How do children fare when they leave your provision?

Auditing strengths and experiences

Although it is clearly important to focus on the needs of children, it is also essential to recognise their strengths, interests and experiences. Whilst these do vary between individual children, you may still find that there are patterns and trends that you can use to build on to further children's learning and development.

Involving parents

An education programme also needs to be constructed with parents in mind. Parents, as we have seen in Chapter 1 (page 12), are usually the most influential people in children's lives, and the way that we work with them impacts significantly on our success as educators. This means that when we are creating an education programme, it is worth thinking about how we will involve parents.

Reflection points

- From your own assessments of groups of children in your setting, what are the areas of strengths?

- Are there any common interests and experiences that groups of children share?

Reflection points

- How can parents be helped to understand the journey that their child will take in your setting?

- What strategies will be employed to involve parents and also to gain feedback from parents?

The children in this setting love to cook and today they are learning about bread.

Working with the early years curriculum

Another factor when planning an education programme is, of course, to do so in the context of the early years curriculum with which you are working. This means that whilst in your long term planning you might want to focus on the experiences, outings, skills and play opportunities that you feel are important for the children you work with, at some point you will need to link these to the curriculum areas or particular outcomes. Luckily, as at present, the early years curricula in each of the home countries is not particularly prescriptive in terms of the exact activities that children must do, this is fairly easy. If for example, you have a long-term programme for children to experience malleable materials and you are working in England, it could be linked to 'physical development', 'understanding the world' and 'expressive arts and design'. On the other hand, if you are working in Wales with the Foundation Phase and had a long-term plan for cooking activities, you might link this to 'personal and social development', 'mathematical development' and 'physical development'.

This child is exploring technology with the support of an adult. Technology is part of the early years curriculum.

It is important that everyone working with the activities in the programme knows the potential learning opportunities and how they link to the curriculum in detail. This is important not only because of the level of detail required if you are inspected, but more significantly, to inform what we draw children's attention to and the skills that we help them gain. A good example of this might be a cooking activity. During some cooking activities, we might focus children on measuring and the language that links to this, but during others we might show children how to use a tool such as grater or a salad spinner.

Reflection points

- How familiar are you with the early years curriculum?

- How easily can you make strong links between the curriculum, specific activities and the needs of individual children?

Summary

If you decide to take the approach I have explored in this chapter in your setting, then at some point you will need to pinpoint the skills, experiences and opportunities that you feel will benefit the children that you work with. In subsequent chapters I look at key areas of development along with strategies and activities that might support children, but for this approach to work well, you will need to think carefully about what you believe is important for the children that you work with.

Here are some questions which might help you on this journey. It is far from being a comprehensive list, but gives a flavour of how strategic planning to help close the gap with children at risk of disadvantage might look.

- How will you introduce a wide knowledge of nursery rhymes to support phonemic awareness?

- How will you support children to develop a love and knowledge of books through sharing them on a 1:1 or 1:2 basis with an adult?

- Would children benefit from cooking activities and, if so, how will you ensure that a range of them are planned?

- How will you introduce a range of malleable materials so that children can learn about texture, shape and form?

- How will you help children learn about the local environment and gain cultural experiences through regular outings?

- How might you use visitors to help children learn more about specific skills, hobbies and job roles?

- How will you introduce children to traditional games such as snap, picture lotto, ludo, which will support their mathematical and cognitive development as well as their social skills?

- How will you plan for a wide range of role play opportunities to extend children's knowledge of different situations and also vocabulary?

- How will you ensure that children develop the necessary hand/eye coordination skills and movements to support self-care as well as early writing?

- What type of self-care skills, including toileting and dressing, need to be focused on and planned for in your setting?

- How will you introduce children to the natural world so that they can recognise and name a range of animals, plants and natural phenomena?

Chapter 4

Widening knowledge, skills and horizons

We can help to close the gap and support children who are at risk of disadvantage by providing them with a wide range of experiences inside and outside the classroom.

'Lucky' children often have access to varied experiences that are accompanied by adult involvement. They may have been taken to a museum or art gallery or have fed the ducks in a park. They may have gone for a walk in the woods or travelled in the car to a wildlife park. 'Lucky' children may also have been involved in some everyday activities such as making biscuits, planting seeds or posting a letter. Such activities are often taken for granted by families, but the reality is that they are all potentially rich learning opportunities for children, that enable them to forge new thoughts as well as to develop high levels of vocabulary.

In this chapter, I am going to explore the importance of varied experiences for children's development as well as considering how these might form the basis of a long-term plan.

Why rich experiences matter

Every experience a child has will shape them in some way. When these experiences are positive and accompanied by adult support, they are great catalysts for learning. They support children's development in a number of ways.

Effects on language development

Children who have had a range of experiences often have higher levels of vocabulary and language than other children. This is because words and phrases are usually learnt in context. Where the context changes in some way, because children are in a new place or seeing something new for example, their language will be shaped accordingly. Children who see an egg being poached will watch the water bubble and the egg changing in texture and colour as a result. They may be prompted to talk about these changes. Assuming that there is a responsive adult, the children may learn specific vocabulary associated with what they are seeing; words such as 'simmer', 'yolk' and 'solid'. In the same way, a child who puts out food for the birds with an adult may learn and use language such as 'bird table', 'seeds' and the names of specific birds.

Effects on cognition

Children who have opportunities to do and see plenty of things are also likely to keep expanding and building on their knowledge. They do this by making connections between previous and new experiences and reflecting on them. As adults working with children, we may hear children's thoughts as they make comments or ask questions. A child putting out bird food might ask

Interesting experiences provide children with opportunities to learn new vocabulary.

These children are playing out their experiences of cooking.

whether birds have to clean their teeth or why the leaves fall from the trees in autumn. By having varied experiences alongside a sensitive adult, children's knowledge and understanding about the world develops.

Effects on play

One of the ways in which the experiences of children are reflected is through their play. Children who have been involved in cooking activities, for example, will often be more accurate in the way they use kitchen utensils in the home area of a setting. In the same way, children who have been involved in shopping trips are more likely to 'browse' in the pretend shop, tender money at the till and talk about what they have bought. The effects on play are not limited to the role play area either. Children who are using a range of other toys and resources will play out their experiences and bring in their knowledge and skills in a variety of ways. Using wooden blocks, they may make plans to build something they have seen or mirror the way that they were involved in constructing flat pack furniture. Where children have fewer experiences, they are often at a disadvantage in their play and although adults can model for them, there is nothing quite like first-hand experience.

Later self-esteem

Some experiences such as picking fruit, posting a letter or cooking a pizza give children opportunities to experience success which helps them to feel 'grown-up'. Having a variety of 'can do' experiences can provide children with a positive self-image, especially when their successes are recognised by their immediate family in addition to the adults working with them.

Aspiration

What you have seen and done and who you have met can all impact on your later choices. 'Lucky' children benefit from a range of experiences and sometimes from the influential networks that surround the family. Research by the Sutton Trust in 2014 showed that the children of more affluent parents tend to benefit from a wide range of activities including music, dance and sport. By giving children a greater number of experiences and opportunities, all children can be introduced to a range of possibilities that in turn, can give them more options.

Effects on later reading

As children progress with their reading, texts often become longer and contain less pictures. This means that children have to make meaning using words alone. Children who have many different experiences are more likely to have a wider vocabulary that can help them to assign meaning to texts, and memories that they can draw on to imagine different scenes and scenarios. For children who have had fewer opportunities to develop their vocabulary , and have limited experiences, these books can feel quite alien.

Effects on writing

Children who have had wide experiences, usually have more to draw on in their writing. They have memories of where they have been, what they have done and what they felt. For these 'lucky' children, writing about the weekend, holidays or imagining a new situation is a straightforward proposition and they often have plenty to 'say'.

Planning for experiences

It is worth spending some time thinking about what experiences you would like all children in your setting to have had by the time they leave you. There is no official list of experiences or opportunities written into the EYFS or any other early years curriculum in the UK, which is ideal because you will be able to focus on the individual needs of the children in your setting. If you are part of a staff team, it is worth having a discussion with your colleagues about the types of experiences that they think will be worthwhile and of course, enjoyable for children. You may also find it helpful to talk to parents too, as their involvement and interest in the activities planned will increase the developmental benefit. You may find that views will differ as, no doubt, the type of activities and outings will be a reflection on what we as individuals experienced during our childhood or what we have done with our own children. When planning for experiences, you might find it helpful to consider the following topics.

Start with the children

It can be worth thinking about the experiences that children may have already had. They are likely, for example, to have visited a supermarket or have been clothes shopping. Consider revisiting the same places, so that children can show us what they already know and to allow us to expand on their learning. Equally, we may also find that through our conversations with children, and through our observations, we can plan experiences alongside them. It may be that children who have enjoyed Eric Carle's book *The Very Hungry Caterpillar* would be interested in going out for a caterpillar hunt in the spring, or we could send away some cocoons for hatching.

Reflection points

- What type of experiences do you feel that children in your setting may have already had?

- How do you record these experiences to help with long-term planning?

- What type of experiences may be of benefit to children in your setting?

Involve families

We might also find that some individual children's families have hobbies and skills that can be used as starting points and can be developed and 'rolled out' to other children. You could send a letter, put up a poster, or simply talk to parents and guardians to gather ideas about how to incorporate their hobbies into your learning programme. Many adults do not realise that their occupation, hobbies or the skill that they have will be of interest to children.

Use own/staff interests

In the same way as we should involve families, we should also think about what we as adults do and enjoy that might be of interest to children. In particular, a key person needs to think about how they might introduce children to new experiences and information based on their own interests, e.g. by putting on some salsa music if they attend a salsa class.

Local outings

It can be tempting when planning a programme of experiences and activities to focus on the 'one off' big outings. Whilst these can be of huge interest to children, I am also a great fan of looking at what is in the immediate vicinity. It may be that there are allotments nearby, a waterway or a local museum. Although children may drive or walk past these places every day, not all children will have experienced them. There are clear advantages to thinking locally and not only in terms of cost. Local places are often easy to get to and accommodating. This means that you might be able to arrange more than one visit, which in turn allows for children to keep on developing their interests and learning. Parents are also more likely to come with you on a trip if it's local and may also consider returning alone with their children. By thinking locally, you may also be able to take out smaller groups of children at a time, which may allow children to be more active during the visit.

Visiting local places can support children's learning.

Local area ideas

Have you thought of visiting any of the following?

- ★ Allotment
- ★ Hairdresser
- ★ Supermarket
- ★ Nail bar
- ★ Post Office
- ★ Charity shop
- ★ Parks and gardens
- ★ Bus depot
- ★ Doctor's/vet surgery

- ★ Train station
- ★ Library
- ★ Pet shop
- ★ Garden centre
- ★ Museum
- ★ Carpet shop
- ★ Leisure centre
- ★ Newsagent
- ★ Art gallery

- ★ Hardware store
- ★ Car dealer/garage
- ★ Takeaway restaurant
- ★ Estate agent
- ★ Key cutter/shoe repairer
- ★ Haberdasher/curtain shop.

Reflection points

- What is available in your local area that may be of interest to children?

- How might you organise a visit to a place of interest?

Inviting visitors to your setting

Bringing visitors into settings is another way in which we can provide children with new experiences. You will find that there are a host of people who have something to show or talk to children about. Public services such as police officers and the fire service are known for their goodwill in this area, but also try local businesses such as opticians, estate agents and vets. You should also consider inviting in visitors who have a skill, but are not necessarily professionals such as people who play sport or play a musical instrument. Children can also be fascinated by people who collect or restore things.

Visitors can help to widen children's experiences.

Who could be a good visitor?

Have you thought of any of these examples of people who may be able to share experiences with children?

* Musicians
* Hairdressers
* Artists
* Health care professionals, e.g. opticians, midwives
* Collectors, e.g. of stamps, coins, figurines, letters…
* Bee keepers
* Sewers, knitters and potters

* Sports people
* Architects and builders
* Retired people
* Gardeners
* Chimney sweeps
* Dog walkers/dog groomers/breeders of animals
* Accountants, insurance brokers.

Experiences within the setting

There are many experiences that, with a little thought and some extra resources, we can plan within the setting. These are often overlooked, but interestingly not only do they develop children's knowledge and skills, but they are often hugely empowering.

Cooking

Food is an integral part of life. Cooking is not just an activity that children enjoy, but it is also an amazing way of helping children to acquire skills, concepts and knowledge. Ideally, it is worth drawing up a cooking programme that builds on children's skills as well as tastes. I know of one setting that prioritises cooking with children and ensures that every child cooks each week. Not only do children enjoying the activity, but parents are involved as the step-by-step photographic recipe card is also sent home. Parents are also invited in to help or to contribute ideas.

Whatever you decide to put into a cooking programme, it would be helpful to minimise recipes involving high levels of sugar, and to look for fairly low cost ingredients that are easily available in the local area. As with any cooking or food activity, it is important to understand the dietary needs of children including religious and medical ones.

There are many ways to implement a cooking programme in your setting. You can organise a cooking programme to introduce new foods or you could consider planning a programme based on building children's skill levels. The table over the page shows some examples of skills and also foods that can be made, many of which do not require a lot of equipment, although of course, all activities will need adult support and supervision.

Cooking skill	Types of dishes/foods
Washing	Washing items for a salad or fruit salad, e.g. lettuce, tomatoes, fruit
Peeling by hand	Making fruit salads Shelling peas Shelling broad beans
Spreading	Making sandwiches Putting topping on to pizzas Spreading soft cheese onto celery sticks
Stirring	Smoothies Cheese scones Porridge Salad dressing
Kneading	Bread Chapatis Pizza bases
Rolling out	Quiche Lorraine Cheese straws Pizza
Cracking eggs	Quiche Lorraine Poached eggs
Grating	Cheese on toast Carrot salad
Cutting using cutters	Cheese scones Slices of bread
Cutting with knives	Feta cheese and cucumber salad
Filling	Pitta bread sandwiches
Boiling (under supervision)	Boiled eggs Potatoes Rice Pasta

Domestic experiences

Young children often enjoy taking part in everyday household experiences. Two-year-olds in particular, seem to be very interested in helping adults with household chores. Many household chores are fantastic learning experiences for children as they encourage talk and help develop children's fine motor skills and can encourage confidence. What adults see as a chore, children can often see as fascinating, e.g. many two- and three-year-olds love sweeping up with a dustpan and brush. Interestingly, 'domestic' duties are a traditional part of education systems such as Montessori and Steiner.

T!P

Domestic experiences

Here are some examples of 'domestic' experiences that seem to appeal to children while also helping them to take ownership of the environment.

* Cleaning shoes

* Washing and drying up beakers and plates

* Sorting laundry into colours ready for washing

* Wiping down and drying tables

* Hanging up clothes onto hangers

* Polishing metal objects e.g. brass

* Folding clothes neatly

* Washing windows

* Sweeping a yard or patio using a broom

* Sweeping using a dustpan and brush

* Sorting out and being involved in labelling resources

* Watering plants.

These children are learning about plants.

Gardening

Most settings have spaces where practitioners can create gardening opportunities for children. This can be anything from deep window boxes to specific areas of the grounds. In some local areas, it may also be possible to rent an allotment so that gardening can take place on a larger scale. Children can learn a lot from gardening, including knowledge about food, nature, seasons and also simple biology. Gardening can also act as a stepping stone to help children investigate using ICT, e.g. with an adult researching the best seeds to plant, when to prune or deadhead flowers. For gardening activities to be effective, it is important that sufficient preparation is put in place as half-hearted attempts where plants do not thrive can be demoralising for children.

Gardening with children

Here are some of the factors that need to be considered before embarking on gardening projects with children. It is always worth contacting keen gardeners or organisations such as the Royal Horticultural Society (www.rhs.org.uk) for advice. Planning and preparing gardening opportunities can also be a great opportunity for children to carry out an investigation with you.

Sun	Where does the sun rise and fall in your setting? • Check how much sunshine the plants or seeds need before you plant them.
Soil type	What type of soil do you have? • Check what type of soil plants or seeds need. You should also check the depth of soil that they will need if you are using containers. • Find out how to improve the soil.
Drainage and watering	How well does the soil drain? • Many plants need good drainage as roots rot when they become water logged. • There are many ways to improve drainage including adding holes to containers, putting down gravel and adding fibrous materials such as compost. How much water do plants need? • In general, small containers dry out quickly and therefore large containers are usually better.
Height	What height will plants grow and will they need supporting? • e.g. Runner beans need a frame but French beans do not.
Cropping	When will vegetables and fruit be ready for cropping? • How does this link to terms or sessions when children will be available?
Safety	Is the plant a potential danger? • Some plants may have foliage that is poisonous. Always check out whether a plant is potentially dangerous to children.

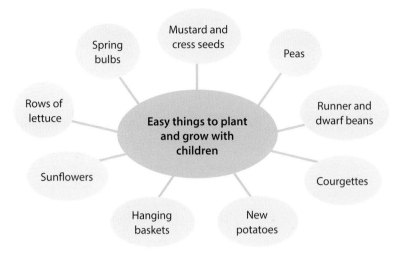

Easy things to plant and grow with children

- Mustard and cress seeds
- Spring bulbs
- Peas
- Rows of lettuce
- Runner and dwarf beans
- Sunflowers
- Courgettes
- Hanging baskets
- New potatoes

Pets/animals

Many children do not have access to pets, especially those who live in urban areas or rented accommodation. Petting, caring and observing pets can be very interesting for children. Ideally, it would be great if every setting had a pet, and I have visited settings that have had everything from chickens to land snails. If you do not currently have a pet, there is plenty of advice available from animal charities that will help you to choose and understand the welfare requirements and how they apply to your setting. Choosing a pet could be a great learning investigation opportunity for children too.

If this is not possible for your setting, think instead of organising for pets to come in. The charity, 'Guide Dogs for the Blind' will often visit settings as part of their fundraising and awareness work. You may also be able to contact a police dog handler who could come in. There are also commercial companies that will bring exotic animals for the day or you can hire out hatching chicks complete with an incubator. You could also contact parents or other people within the local community that have pets, however you must remember to complete a risk assessment first.

Children benefit from having access to animals.

Music

With a growing focus on academic subjects within the educational programme, it is important that we do not overlook the importance of the arts. This is why helping children to meet people who paint, draw, model or sew is important as it can inspire children and open their eyes to a range of possibilities that can be built on within the setting. One of the areas that you might like to focus on in terms of widening children's knowledge in a planned way is music. Whilst rhymes and songs are regularly sung in most settings, you might like to think about how you introduce children to different types of music such as jazz, choral, reggae, classical and folk. Different types of music reflect cultures, moods and emotions and using technology, we should easily be able to expand children's experiences of sound as well as our own.

A good starting point might be to think about the music that children are already hearing and enjoying and then to explore other sounds and rhythms that can widen their experience. It is also important to identify when music can be played during the day. Background music that is not related to the session can deter younger children from talking, and older children may not gain from it because they are not focusing in on it.

Planning an education programme around experiences

Experiences and opportunities for children do not just magically appear, they take planning. Therefore, it is worth thinking strategically and creating a long-term plan. Of course, a plan is just that, and changes can be made as new opportunities arise or the needs and interests of children change. If your setting has children over three years, but also children as young as age two for example, the plan will also need to consider their skill and developmental level to ensure that they gain maximum benefit.

There are many ways in which you might construct a plan, but you could divide the types of experiences into three broad categories:

1. Visitors, including family members

2. Places to visit

3. Experiences that can be carried out within the setting.

These photographs are helping the child to recall their memory of this experience.

Making the most of experiences

As it takes both time and planning to organise a rolling programme of experiences for children, it is important to maximise the impact of each experience. This means thinking of ways to help children make and extend connections in their learning beyond the immediate moment. There are many ways of doing this and these should be incorporated into the actual planning of the experience at the outset. They include:

- Using photographs taken at the time (either by children or adults)

- Making books or displays about the experience

- Using the experience to help children find out more afterwards by researching online or using books, e.g. looking at maps, websites about cooking, wildlife

- Developing role and small world play opportunities with children based on the experiences

- Involving parents at the time or, if this is not possible, sharing with them via social media, websites or photographs of the experience

- Using experiences to encourage early writing and mark making by, e.g. making books, creating annotations for photographs or sending e-mails or letters to thank those in the community who were involved in the experience

- Leading and encouraging storytelling about the experience, e.g. 'This is the story of the day that we made porridge'

- Placing relevant props or artefacts for children to handle and talk about in the environment

- Encouraging children to reflect on their experiences and to archive these, e.g. make film clips of children explaining what they have done or pointing to where they have planted seeds.

Reflection points

- Do you have a long-term plan for 'experiences' inside and outside of your setting?

- Do you map these to your early years framework, e.g. EYFS, Curriculum for Excellence, Foundation Phase?

- How many different opportunities will children experience in the time that they are with you?

- How do you involve parents and the community in planning and implementing experiences for children?

- How do you ensure that opportunities for learning are optimised during and after each experience?

Revisiting and grouping experiences

The way that children process and explore different experiences will depend on several factors, including their level of enjoyment and interest, but also their age and developmental stage. When planning a programme, it will be worth thinking about revisiting some of the experiences, as this will allow children to make further and more complex connections based on their growing understanding of the world. It may also be worth, when planning, to group some experiences together so that they build on from one another, e.g. a visit to an allotment, followed by a cooking activity that involves foods that the children have seen growing.

Summary

In this chapter, I have explored the role experiences play in supporting children's language development, cognition and understanding of the world. I have also looked at how children bring their experiences in to their child-initiated play. I have also given suggestions about the type of experiences that might benefit children, although one of the messages from this chapter is that every setting will need to consider what experiences might be important for their own children. As a result of reading this chapter, you might decide to develop a programme of experiences and incorporate them into some form of long-term planning. As part of your planning, it will also be useful to cross-reference experiences to the areas of the EYFS or whatever early years framework you use.

Chapter 5

Creating an environment for personal, social and emotional development

We can only help to successfully close the gap if children's personal, social and emotional development (PSED) is taken into consideration. Children's PSED plays a huge role in their ability to connect to others, thrive in a group setting and develop the skills of self-regulation. It is a complex area of development in which there are many areas to consider. These include temperament, attachment, cognition and language as well as the environment itself. 'Lucky' children in the early years are well on their way to developing strong self-esteem, a sense of efficacy and empathy for others. They can also self-regulate their behaviour which allows them to adapt to new experiences as well as to respond appropriately to others. However, when working with disadvantaged children, we need to focus on their PSED if we are to help close the gap in terms of their later attainment. This chapter examines practical ways to support children's PSED.

From age three, most children can start to take turns when playing simple games.

Factors affecting children's PSED

There are a range of factors that can impact on children's PSED. Some of these factors are purely developmental, others are linked to parent-child attachment as well as experiences.

Language and cognition

The skills relating to self-regulation, including managing impulses, are developmental in nature. This means that most young two-year-olds, regardless of all external factors, are likely to be impulsive and find social activities such as sharing and waiting for a turn extremely difficult. This is because the parts of the brain that deal with planning and analysis are not yet sufficiently developed to help children exercise control. In fact, these parts of the brain continue to develop beyond the teenage years. Language also plays a part as it underpins thinking and reasoning. It helps children to internalise

responses that adults used to help them understand and cope with their emotions over time, e.g. an adult says empathetically to a child, 'I know you wanted to have a turn now, but if you wait for a moment, it will soon be your go.'

Self-regulation

As self-regulation is highly linked to developmental factors, when developing routines, expectations of behaviour and activities, it is important to understand typical age-related behaviours. When adults have unrealistic expectations or create routines that are inappropriate for young children, there is a danger that everyone may become frustrated. It is also worth noting that children with lower language levels than expected for their age are more likely to behave in a similar way to younger children and therefore they may need more support and help.

A guide to typical age-related self-regulation

18–24 months	Can concentrate on an activity they have chosen but may not take any direction from an adult.
	Can do some simple turn-taking in activities alongside an adult, e.g. rolling a ball.
2–3 years	Is beginning to listen, but is easily distracted.
	Listens when talk is addressed directly to him/her.
	Likelihood of tantrums when unable to get their own way.
	Has little understanding of dangers.
	Has little understanding of sharing toys or an adult's attention.
3–4 years	Is starting to modulate emotions and impulses sufficiently to play with others.
	Is able to understand others' emotions.
	Can play co-operatively with others.
	Knows behavioural rules, e.g. to walk indoors or to wait for their turn in a game or other activity.
	Knows how to 'use' emotions to meet their needs or to 'negotiate', e.g. crying to get a parent to change his/her mind.
	Needs to look in order to listen and attend.
4–5 years	Is starting to be able to control some emotions.
	Is able to wait before making choices to see whether there may be a better choice, e.g. not just taking the first thing offered.
	Understands that some behaviour is inappropriate.
	Able to concentrate and maintain attention on goals, e.g. finishing a jigsaw puzzle.
	Is able to listen whilst simultaneously engaged in another activity.

Sleep

Whilst development plays a significant part in children's ability to self-regulate, manage emotions and to respond appropriately to others, so too does sleep! Children who are under-sleeping are more likely to be irritable, have aggressive outbursts and have difficulty concentrating. Interestingly, the signs of attention deficit hyperactivity disorder (ADHD) are very similar to the signs of sleep deprivation. It is always worth considering whether lack of sleep could be a factor in those children who have difficulties with their social skills and self-regulation. Although all children do need slightly different amounts of sleep, the chart below is based on current information from the NHS and shows the typical hours of sleep needed for different ages.

Reflection points

● Do you provide effective provision for children to have naps?

● How do you share information with parents about typical sleep needs of children?

● Do you know where you can signpost parents who are having difficulty managing their child's sleep? (See also Chapter 1, page 26)

How much sleep?

The following information is taken from the NHS choices website (**www.nhs.uk/Livewell/Childrenssleep**).

3 months	daytime:	4 to 5 hours
	night time:	10 to 11 hours
6 months	daytime:	3 hours
	night time:	11 hours
9 months	daytime:	2 hours, 30 minutes
	night time:	11 hours
12 months	daytime:	2 hours, 30 minutes
	night time:	11 hours, 30 minutes
2 years	daytime:	1 hour 30 minutes
	night time:	11 hours
3 years	daytime:	0 to 45 minutes
	night time:	11 hours, 30 minutes to 12 hours
4 years	night time:	11 hours 30 minutes
5 years	night time:	11 hours

Temperament

Temperament and personality are thought to be partly inherited, but also highly influenced by experiences and interaction with others. In children's earliest years, their personality is still developing, but early traits can often be observed. Most parents and practitioners can see that some children are more sociable and outgoing and feel the need to be with adults and children. Other children are more self-contained. In children's earliest years it is important not to label them as 'shy' or 'extrovert' as this can be constraining, however it is worth observing children's specific preferences. This may mean that some children will be very quick to take an interest in other children while others may take their time.

Attachment and responsive adults

Children's experiences of attachment play a significant part in supporting the development of their social skills, ability to manage emotions and also self-regulation. Children benefit from having strong attachments with their parents or primary caregivers. Attachment is now recognised as being very important in babies and toddlers. It appears to give them a template for how relationships work, feelings of empathy and also how to cope with stress. Attachment is also important in the development of a child's self-identity. Consistent positive responses from primary attachments help children construct a self-identity based on feelings of worth. The reasons why some children do not have strong attachments and why some adults find it difficult to be responsive to their children are complex. They are sometimes linked to events out of parents' control, e.g. post-natal depression, a significant bereavement, childhood abuse.

As attachment issues clearly play a significant part in children's development, it is worth researching the issues that surround attachment and, where necessary, gaining professional advice about how best to support a child.

Reflection points

- Do you know where you signpost parents when there are concerned about attachment?

- Do you know where to find information to support children where there are attachment difficulties?

Strong attachments to parents have a protective effect on children's emotional security.

Supporting children's emotional well-being

The starting point for supporting children's emotional well-being and helping them develop social skills is through their key person. All young children need a key person for their emotional health and also, as we will see in other chapters, to support their learning. The key person acts as a child's bedrock. They should be able to tune into their moods and show unconditional regard and empathy towards them. This is important because if children have not experienced care and empathy, they will struggle to show it to others. This is one of the reasons why there is a close link between emotional and social development.

Parenting style

There is no such thing as a perfect parent but there is much evidence to suggest that some parenting styles are more likely to help children's emotional and social development than others. Children benefit if their parents are confident in their role, and are responsive to them. These parents are also able to put in place age or stage appropriate boundaries and adapt their style of parenting to the changing developmental needs of their children. This style of parenting is called 'authoritative' parenting.

It is important to separate parenting style from attachment as some parent-child attachments can be strong, yet parents may not set consistent boundaries. It is also worth noting that where a child lives with more than one parent or primary caregiver, there can also be inconsistency in style between them. Whilst some degree of difference is to be expected as we all respond to children differently, it would appear that significant inconsistencies and conflicts over parenting styles is not helpful for children.

The role of the key person

The role of the key person becomes doubly important for children who need extra stability and consistency. The key person will act as a mentor and guide providing some children with an additional template showing them how to interact with others and deal with difficult situations. (See Chapter 1, page 19)

Whilst children who have had consistency and stability in their lives are often able to easily form a new relationship with their key person, this is not always the case with all children. This means that a key person will need to be patient, consistent and have sufficient experience to be able to forge a strong relationship with a child. It is also likely that some children will show a range of challenging behaviours, which in part is linked to their subconscious need to 'stress test' the relationship. It is therefore important to think about how the key person system is organised in your setting and how key persons are allocated to individual children.

Reflection points

● How do you signpost support for parents who are interested in exploring other ways of parenting?

● How do you ensure that the way that you work within the setting mirrors 'authoritative' parenting?

Key person-child relationship

To effectively help children grow and develop, a significant amount of time needs to be invested in the key person-child relationship. This means that thought has gone into how sessions are organised to ensure that the key person-child relationship can develop. We also need to think about the duration of the relationship. For a child who has frequently seen significant adults come and go in their lives, stability of a key person is important and so it may be worth considering whether a key person can move with their key child throughout their time in the setting. If this is not possible, they should ideally remain involved in some way with the child and also help the child to make the transition to another key person.

Safety net

Although it is important that children do have a strong key person relationship, a safety net has to be provided for when that person is not available, e.g. when they are on holiday or on a training course. The terms 'co-key person' and 'buddy' are often used to describe a system where another adult is able to take the key person's place. Such systems are essential, as the child may feel abandoned if their key person is not available. For a co-key person or buddying system to work well, it is important that the child spends enough time with the second adult on a regular basis in order to form a strong relationship with them too. It is likely that between two adults, a child is going to have a preference for one over the other. This is usual, as most families would say that their child's key relationships are hierarchical.

Children need time to develop a relationship with their key person.

Reflection points

- How are key persons allocated to children in your setting?

- How much training and advice is available about being a key person?

- How much time do individual children have with their key person during a session?

- How do you ensure that you provide continuity of care when the key person is not available?

- How do you provide long-term relationships for children who have had disrupted relationships in the past?

Building a positive self-image

Self-esteem is the level of self-worth that individuals feel about themselves. The process of developing self-esteem begins in early childhood when children start to construct a self-image – 'what am I like?'. Later on in their primary years, children then develop an 'ideal self'. The 'ideal self' is the person that you would like to be. It is thought that a high self-esteem is gained when children's self-image matches their 'ideal self' closely.

By understanding the ways in which children construct their self-image, we can work out how best to work with them.

Registering responses

Children learn about themselves by registering other people's responses to them. All children, including babies, are sensitive to others' tone of voice, body language and facial expression. Children who, on the whole, have warm responses from adults and other children are more likely to learn that they are 'likeable'.

Hearing what others say

What children are told and also what they overhear also helps them to learn about themselves. It is thought that by 18 months, most children know, for example, whether they are a boy or a girl. This is learnt before children have any notion of biological/sexual difference. They learn this by adults saying things such as, 'There's a good boy', or 'Who's my special little girl?'. The way in which children develop their self-identity by listening to what others say to them and about them is one reason why statements such as 'naughty girl' are not thought to be helpful. From this type of remark, a child might come to the conclusion that they are wholly naughty.

Reflection points

- How warm and affectionate are adults towards children in your setting?

- Does every child in the setting hear frequent positive messages?

- What statements are used when dealing with unwanted behaviour?

- Do you talk to parents or each other about children's progress or behaviour within earshot of children?

What is this child learning about herself from the response of this adult?

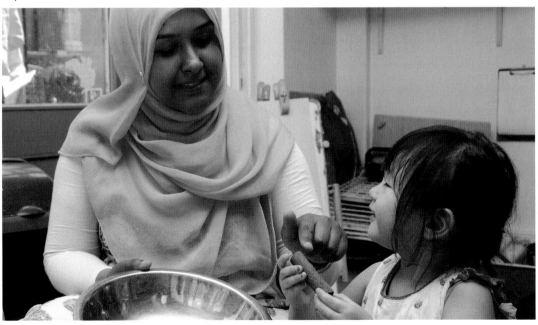

Comparing themselves with others

Later in childhood, usually from around five-years-old, children learn about themselves by comparing themselves with others. This is the stage at which children often make statements such as, 'I can run fast, but Seth is the fastest in our class!'. Children also increasingly note how other children are treated by adults and draw inferences from this, e.g. one child may notice if their friend appears to receive more praise or smiles from an adult than them.

Self-efficacy

Children also learn from their experiences. One feature of this is their understanding of whether they are inherently 'capable'. The term 'self-efficacy' is used to describe this aspect of our self-image. A strong sense of self-efficacy means that children come to new experiences expecting that they will have the capacity to achieve and so are more likely to persevere. It is thought that self-efficacy begins very early on and is helped by adults encouraging children to do things for themselves, e.g. the baby who is allowed to self-feed rather than be a passive recipient of food. (See Chapter 10, page 177.) The response of adults to children's attempts to try out new things and to do things from themselves is important. If adults become repeatedly irritated or take back a task, children may learn from this that they are not capable. On the other hand, where adults are positive and guide children in ways that make them feel autonomous, children will develop a strong sense of self-efficacy. There are many ways in which we can help children's self-efficacy including:

- Encouraging children to develop self-care skills

- Giving children stage-/age-appropriate choices

- Giving children stage-/age-appropriate responsibilities, e.g. filling up a bird feeder

- Allowing children to play a part in grown-up tasks such as holding the dustpan or holding the tape when a book is being repaired.

Reflection points

- What opportunities are there in your setting to encourage children's sense of self-efficacy?

- How do you provide encouragement for children to try out new things?

- How do you plan stage-/age-appropriate opportunities for children to become autonomous?

- How do you ensure as children develop that they are given increasing responsibility and opportunities to be autonomous?

Self-care skills can help children develop a sense of self-efficacy

Supporting children's social skills

The development of social skills is, as we have seen at the start of the chapter, linked to development as well as to other factors. It is important therefore to have a good understanding of individual children's development, especially in relation to language, in order to plan and support children's social skills. Children whose social skills are weak tend to be either neglected or rejected by their peers. This can impact on their confidence and can result in aggressive or frustrated behaviours. In some cases, children may also become withdrawn. There are many skills that children need to learn if they are to be accepted by their peers and develop friendships. They include turn-taking, sharing and learning to join in play. Many of these are linked to children's ability to self-regulate (see page 78).

Turn-taking

Learning to take turns is an important social and communication tool. Most children learn turn-taking as babies through playing games such as peek-a-boo. For some children, turn-taking needs to be reinforced and encouraged. When this is the case, it is important to make sure that the turn-taking situation or activity is within the child's capability. This might mean turn-taking between an adult and child to start with before the child practises turn-taking with a couple of other children. Children who find it hard to take turns will need plenty of encouragement and praise. Examples of simple turn-taking activities include:

- Building a tower of bricks together
- Rolling a ball back and forth
- Completing a simple jigsaw – one piece at a time
- Passing around a plate of snacks
- Small circle games, e.g. make a sound with a shaker and then pass the shaker on.

Sharing

An important social skill for children to gain is the ability to share resources. Most children are able to do this from three-years-old, although when children are tired or there are insufficient resources, this can become tricky. We can help children to learn this skill by modelling how to share, e.g. offering a jigsaw piece to a child, or asking a child directly to share something with us and then praising the child afterwards. Children also need to learn about why sharing is important and how it might feel if someone does or does not share something with you. It is important that early sharing experiences are easy for children and that they are not being asked to share something that is particularly precious to them.

Joining play

Some children find it hard to join play or maintain play with other children. It is worth observing children in order to understand why. Some children try to take over the direction of play rather than join in with others, whilst others are too boisterous or snatch things. For children with good levels of language, it is worth coaching them about how to join play. You could start by encouraging children simply to stand and watch others play before copying their movements. Children also need to be coached so that they learn that they cannot always direct the play or, in the case of a game, win. It is worth using stories or puppets to talk about what is 'nice play'.

Reflection points

- What activities do you use to model and encourage children to take turns and share?

- Do you observe children as they try to join play?

- How do you support children who find playing with others difficult?

Consistent routines help children to learn self-regulation skills.

Creating an environment to support self-regulation

Self-regulation is an umbrella term for a range of skills that support children's ability to learn, but also to control their impulses. There is some research to suggest that low levels of self-regulation can impact significantly on children's attainment. Being able to control impulses is important in relation to social skills such as sharing and taking turns. There are several ways in which we can help children acquire self-regulation.

Stability and consistency of approach

'Lucky' children have plenty of stability and consistency in their lives. They quite literally, as well as metaphorically, 'know where they are'. They know who will be there for them, what is expected of them and crucially how adults are likely to respond to them. This in turn allows them to feel physically as well as emotionally safe. These are prerequisite conditions for learning but also for them to know how to engage with others and be able to self-regulate. For children who, for a variety of reasons have

not experienced stability and consistency in the earliest years, there is a higher likelihood of stress-related responses including impulsivity. It is thought that children who have been very unsettled are likely to be more sensitive to stress and so responses including 'flight or fight' behaviours are more likely to be seen.

One of the key ways in which we can support children is to look at the many ways in which we create a stable and consistent environment.

Routines and structure

Routines are important for all children, particularly when they first join a setting. Routines help children to orientate themselves as they know what will happen, where they need to be and what they need to do. For children who have not experienced a settled existence, routines are particularly important in reducing their stress levels. It is therefore worth creating some additional routines for individual children, which ideally should be carried out alongside their key person. There is added advantaged to having extra individual routines in terms of children's language levels (see Chapter 6, page 98)

Start of the session

When working with parents it is helpful to construct a handover routine. The start of the session can be particularly tricky for children and it is important that it gets off to a smooth start. The child has to reconnect with their key person and also the setting and its expectations. For some children this takes a little time and if they are not guided, there is a danger that the first half hour of their time in the session will be characterised by impulsive behaviours.

There is no single way of helping children to glide into a setting, but the following can work well with some children:

- Staying outdoors with the key person and playing a predictable game, e.g. throwing beanbags

- Changing clothes, e.g. putting on a role play outfit

- Saying hello to the setting's pet

- Sharing a favourite book with the key person.

During the session

As well as having some clear routines for all children during the session, such as at songs and rhyme time, mealtime or snack, some children may need several further 'personal' routines during the session itself. It may be that they come alongside their key person to help prepare snacks, or work with the key person and a couple of other children during tidy up time. It is worth observing children during a session to see whether there are any patterns in their behaviours and responses that would indicate that an additional mini-routine or two, where they can connect with their key person might be necessary. This may be particularly worthwhile in settings where there are a large number of children, e.g. over 20.

Children benefit from a going home routine.

Preparing for the end of the session

In the same way that we may help children to glide into the session, we may also need to think about how we help children at the end of the session. This is sometimes a period when children may show responses such as refusing to get their coat or lashing out. This often happens when children feel that there is a 'power vacuum' between the different adults – parent and practitioner. It is therefore worth working with parents to agree on a routine to help the child leave and also to agree who will guide the child if challenging behaviour is shown.

Reflection points

- Do you create additional routines for individual children in your setting?

- How do you help individual children settle into the session each day?

- Do you observe children's activity and slot in additional routines during the session?

- How do you help children prepare for the end of the session?

Consistency matters

An important factor in supporting children's self-regulation is to ensure that there is a consistency in expectations and adult responses. This means that a whole-setting approach to how to support individual children as well as groups of children needs to be put in place.

Consistent expectations

There are many unwritten expectations within early years settings. It may be that there are separate aprons for different activities, or that children wash their hands before snack time. These relatively small things can be difficult for some children who have difficulty with self-regulation. A child who can see that it is snack time may want to go straight to the food rather than to wash their hands first. Learning to wait or to do a preliminary task can support the development of self-regulation, but children may need adult support to do this and they will also need to have opportunities to practise this consistently. Ways to help children may include:

- Using a step-by-step visual timetable so that the child can see the journey

- Adult support in the form of encouragement or distraction

- Repeated positive recognition.

For children who have low levels of self-regulation, it is important to recognise that a lot of support and positive recognition will need to be provided. Expectations of how long a child can wait or the number of preliminary tasks needs to be fair for the child's stage of development. Whilst most three-year-olds can wait for their turn before helping themselves to a snack, it might work best if a child with low levels of self-regulation is placed so that they are second in line and therefore does not have to control their impulses for very long.

It is important that everyone in the setting understands the specific expectations for individual children and the rationale for why certain systems are in place. This is not about lowering your standards in terms of behaviour, or letting children get away with things. Instead it is about taking a step-by-step approach that is realistic and attainable. Hopefully, by having consistent but fair expectations, and whilst working on any areas of developmental delay, children can then make swift progress.

> ### Reflection points
>
> - How do you ensure that expectations for individual children are realistic?
>
> - How do you help children understand what is required of them during the session?

Consistent responses

In the same way that we need clear and fair expectations, it is also important that adults provide consistent responses. In settings where there are several adults, clear strategies and agreements need to be put in place about how to respond to individual children. Responses need to be stage-appropriate. For children with low levels of language, consistent responses may involve a significant amount of non-verbal communication, including showing approval using clapping or smiling as well as modelling behaviours. It is also important to agree on consistent responses when impulsive or aggressive behaviours are taking place. These again need to be stage-appropriate and may include:

- Distraction
- Reminder
- Warning
- Removal of equipment
- Ignoring behaviour, e.g. adult turning their back on the situation and looking away
- Modelling alternative behaviour
- Taking the child away from the situation and providing an alternative activity.

For children with low levels of language, long explanations or post-mortems are ineffective. This is because children's ability to process the information being given by the adult is limited. Children with low levels of language tend instead to focus on facial expression, gesture and actions.

Reflection points

- How do you ensure that responses towards children are consistent?

- How do you manage unwanted behaviour with consistency?

Temptation

Children with low levels of self-regulation are likely to be highly impulsive. They may also find it hard to delay gratification and so are likely to 'do now, think later'. This means that great thought has to be given into how to create an environment that does not constantly bounce them into situations that they cannot deal with. Simply telling a child who has low levels of language and self-regulation not to touch something is not an effective strategy. Instead, we may need to audit and adapt the environment and remove items that are potentially 'tempting'. In some ways this approach is the equivalent of a parent 'childproofing' a space when they have a toddler. As some children are effectively at the toddler stage in terms of self-regulation, it makes sense to work in this way. This is not a negative approach, it is a proactive one. It allows the child to operate in the environment in a positive way and prevents adults from being reactive.

Developing children's concentration

Concentration is linked to self-regulation. Therefore, it is an important area to focus on as children who have limited concentration find it hard to learn. Although concentration is partly developmental, but we can still create environments that can support children's concentration.

Small spaces – reducing sensory distractions

Large spaces that have a range of colour, noise and texture work well for most children but they are often distracting for children with low self-regulation. Help these children concentrate by is to creating smaller, calm spaces which are visually neutral. Limiting the number of children allowed in the space at any one time can also be helpful as this will reduce noise and movement. How often you should encourage children to use these spaces will depend on the individual child's needs, but for many children this approach is highly effective, provided that the activity or play opportunity on offer is enjoyable and interesting.

Choice and guidance

One of the benefits of most early years settings is the number of different activities, play opportunities and resources on offer. However, this can be problematic for children who are struggling with concentration. It can result in children who continue to move from one activity to another without actually spending sufficient time on each activity in order to gain from it.

For some children it may be that, along with a smaller space, the choice of play opportunities or the number of resources is limited. Instead of five jigsaw puzzles being available, there is only one which matches the child's skill level. As part of this, an adult may also need to model the use of materials and play alongside children to help them to maintain concentration. This can be effective in helping children to learn to focus and concentrate.

Cosy areas can help children to concentrate.

Reflection points

- Are there children in your setting who find it hard to concentrate and stay with an activity?

- How do you work with these children to help them concentrate?

- Do you provide spaces that help to reduce the number of distractions?

- Are there children who may benefit from having a streamlined approach in terms of the quantity and range of resources available?

- How do adults help children to stay focused?

Coaching for perseverance

As well as concentration, children also need to learn the skills of perseverance. Some children can acquire this without adult support as they have a strong sense of self-efficacy, whereas many children with low self-regulation will need an adult to support them.

A good starting point for this is to make sure that activities, play opportunities and resources are within children's skill level. It is also important to think about children's level of concentration, as an activity or play opportunity that requires 15 minutes of concentration may be too long for some children to manage. Building up 'stamina' and perseverance go hand in hand. Play opportunities or activities that can be broken down into individual steps can be helpful, as not only is there an 'end point', but also children can have a sense of achieving something tangible. It is also important to choose play opportunities or activities that are enjoyable and motivating for the child. Observing what the child has already attempted to do or is interested in can work well. Examples of activities that might be helpful, are:

- Building a sandcastle
- Putting on dressing up clothes
- Doing a jigsaw
- Participating in a cooking activity.

Children may need an adult's support to help them persevere.

Coaching children

A good strategy to help children persevere is to coach them through a task step-by-step. This approach helps prevent children from becoming overwhelmed by an activity. It is advisable to use a conversational rather than instructional tone when speaking to the child, e.g. 'Now you have finished this part, it may be a good idea to look back at the picture.'

To start with, some children will need a lot of praise and encouragement at each step. (Over time, the aim is for the child to reflect on how they are feeling and so learn the skill of self-recognition.) When a child is finding a step in the task difficult, it will be important for the child to learn to persevere and while you may decide to offer help, it is important not to take over. Instead, encourage the child to direct you so that the task remains theirs. If the child has good language skills, you may also use this as an opportunity to help the child learn to reflect by asking questions such as, 'Do you think that this will get easier with practice?'

When a child has finished a task, it is important that recognition of their achievement is given and children are asked to think about how it feels. Interestingly, the more opportunities that children have to finish things and to feel successful, the easier it becomes for them to persevere – especially when adults encourage them to reflect on how they have managed to succeed in the past.

Reflection points

- How do you observe children's level of perseverance?

- How do you coach children to achieve tasks?

- How do you help children to recognise their own perseverance?

Planning and reviewing

A further skill that children need to develop is the ability to plan and make choices. We have already seen that we may need to streamline choices for some children at first, but once children have developed some of the skills of concentration and perseverance, it is important to help them plan. There are plenty of models of how to do this, including the Highscope model of 'Plan, Do and Review' (www.highscope.org), which you may like to research separately.

Helping children to plan and review can take place through a series of questions. This is a useful strategy because it encourages children to learn to use language to express their thoughts which is an example of metacognition skill. Below I have provided an example of how to lead children using series of questions. If you decide to take this approach, it is important to allow them enough processing and thinking time. You may also want to adapt this to meet the language and cognition needs of individual children.

18-24 months	What do you want to do?
	What do you want to happen?
	How will you feel when you have finished?
2-3 years	What will you need? (e.g. resources, space)
	Do you want to do it with someone else?
	Do you need adult help?
	How are you going to overcome obstacles?
	What will you do first?
	What will you do next?
3-4 years	Can you think of anything that may be a problem?
	Is there anything that you will need to think about before starting? (e.g. safety)
4-5 years	So how did it go?
	What were you pleased with?
	How are you feeling?
	What worked well?
	Was there anything that you would change?
	What do you need? (e.g. resource, more practice)
	What are you going to try next time?

Reflection points

- How do you support children's planning skills?

- How do adults in your setting coach children and help them to review their activities and play?

Summary

In this chapter we have looked at the importance of supporting children's personal, social and emotional development. We have considered the factors that might affect children's development in this area including short-term factors, such as sleep, as well as language delay. We have seen that the starting point for this is the quality of the key person relationship and the importance of checking that this relationship develops well. We have also looked at self-regulation because research suggests that this is impacts on children's social development, and their ability to reach their learning potential. Whilst there is increasing pressure on early years settings to show 'progress' in relation to children's learning, taking time to evaluate your setting's approach to children's personal, social and emotional development is incredibly valuable because of the underlying links to attainment.

Chapter 6

Communication and language

In many early years settings closing the attainment gap is linked to improving children's language levels.

Communication and language is key for children's development and therefore should be a prominent area of learning within all early years curricula including the EYFS. 'Lucky' children usually have high levels of language and often exceed the expectations for their age group. This is because they have plenty of opportunities for sensitive and sustained interactions with interested adults. In order to make a difference to children who are at risk of disadvantage, it is essential that we adopt a strategic approach to supporting this area of development within our settings. Working on children's communication and language is one of the key ways in which we can prevent children from underperforming and is also one of the areas of development that is highly influenced by the way that adults work.

In this chapter, I examine the importance of communication and language to children's overall development and suggest ways that staff in early years settings can work strategically to support children whose language may need developing further or extending. In Chapter 7, I will look more specifically at the needs of bilingual children although, as you might expect, there is some overlap.

Why communication and language matters

I have no doubt that children's emotional well-being should always take priority over other areas of development but communication and language is often considered the second most important factor. It is one of those areas where the way adults work with children can have a significant impact on their life chances. For example, vocabulary scores at age 5 are a huge predictor of academic success in later life. This demonstrates that language opens the door to many other areas of development. Strong levels of language are associated with the speed at which children acquire the skills of reading and writing. Communication and language skills also affect children's ability to play with other children and the way in which they play.

Levels of communication and language also impact on children's ability to moderate their behaviours. Children who find it difficult to communicate are likely to become frustrated because they are unable to express their feelings in words or to understand the motives and language of others. In addition, as we will see when we look at cognition and early mathematics (see Chapter 9, page 150), language levels impact on how children perceive the world and whether they are able to use higher level skills such as deduction and problem-solving. Working significantly on communication and language in the early years is therefore key to reducing the potential disadvantage that children may have.

Relationships first

Babies and young children do not learn to talk because it is good for them. They are motivated to communicate and talk because they want to connect with adults and other children. No strategy to boost children's language levels can therefore be effective without taking this into consideration. The quality of relationships that children and adults develop underpins all child development and therefore should be the starting point for practitioners who are aiming to support language skills. There are also a number of language programmes that settings can consider adopting such as ECAT.

Effective key persons

In Chapter 2 (page 32), I looked at the importance of key persons developing a partnership with parents and helping children to have a secure base in the setting. In this chapter, I look at how key persons can support children's communication and language via the emotional connection they have established. Where children have a strong relationship with their key person, the foundations are in place to support communication and language. This is because children talk more to the people that they enjoy being with.

The EYFS and other early years frameworks within the UK require that children have key persons (key workers in Wales). This applies in England to schools both in their nurseries and reception classes. Whilst the inspection arrangements for schools may not focus on the quality of attachments between children and key persons, this should still be a focus for settings because there is a clear link between relationships and language outcomes. Therefore, if you intend to review the language practice and opportunities within your setting it is worth beginning by auditing the quality of individual children's relationships with their key persons.

Being able to talk is a key factor in children's overall development.

A strong key person relationship is important in supporting children's language development.

Auditing 'talking relationships'

Interestingly, it is very straightforward to audit how well the key person relationships are working in practice. When children have strong attachments to adults, they show them through a range of seeking behaviours which may include:

- Looking for their key person on arrival in the setting and wanting to say goodbye at the end of session

- Seeking their key person out for reassurance, e.g. when their parent leaves or if they fall over

- Making physical contact with their key person, e.g. stroking, hugging and holding hands

- Wanting the key person to be involved in their play

- Showing items to their key person, e.g. what the child has found or what the child has made or painted

- Asking the key person to sit next to them or wanting to be physically near their key person.

Proximal attachments

In addition to these seeking behaviours, it is also worth recognising that children under three in particular, need strong levels of attachment. They will show more examples of proximal attachment behaviours, e.g. wanting to be close by and near 'their adult'. This is normal and healthy. It is one of the reasons why parenting of this age range can be such a challenge as children will not 'go off and play'. Instead, they will move themselves and any toys to be closer to their adult. Indeed many parents of two-year-olds will report that they cannot even visit the toilet in their own home without their children coming along too!

If you are working with children aged two and younger, you should audit the level of their attachments very carefully. In particular, you may see the children doing the following:

- Regularly glancing to see where in the room their key person is

- Standing close to the key person and trying to stay nearby them during the session

- Becoming distressed when their key person is out of sight or not available to them

- Pushing away other children or being jealous of the adult showing attention to others

- Waiting by the door for their key person to emerge from another area

- Frequently wanting to be held, hugged or touched.

Touch for young children is a way of gaining reassurance.

The importance of prioritising the key person

As well as providing an emotional/social context where language can take place, there are several practical reasons why it is important to prioritise the key person who is working in the setting.

Frequency of interactions

Forming close relationships with adults usually means that interactions tend to be more frequent and also more sustained. Instead of interactions occurring because adults seek out children, the reverse is true. Children actively choose to go and find their key person because they enjoy being with them. Where children are not used to frequent positive interactions in their home environments, this becomes particularly important to monitor.

Listening and attention

Listening and attention is fundamental and is one of the first areas that speech and language therapists focus on when assessing and developing language programmes for children. When children have a positive relationship with their key person they are motivated to listen and be attentive. This is easy to see in practice as children are likely to make eye contact with adults that they are comfortable with, rather than to look away or down. In the same way, children are more likely to become involved in joint attention (where adult and child focus on the same thing).

Children also benefit because they can quickly 'tune' into how the adult communicates, both in terms of voice, but also expressions and body language.

Understanding children's speech

Typically, young children can be hard to understand – especially when they are first talking. Two-year-olds in particular often delete sounds from words and also replace sounds because their speech is still immature. Combine this with a cold and some language delay and, unless you know a child very well, you may not be able to understand what they are trying to communicate. This in turn can make the child frustrated, and if a pattern emerges of not being understood, some children may lose the motivation to try and talk.

Pitching language at the right level

A strong key person is likely to pitch their interactions with the child at the right level. This is because they know what the child knows. They know how the child usually responds and also what the child is interested in. This affects the language that they use, how much processing time they give the child and the style of communication that they use.

Assessment and tracking progress

As we will see later in the chapter, precise assessment of a child's communication and language is essential in planning activities and supporting progress. Knowing children well helps you to assess them and also recognise their progress.

Celebrating progress

Finally, we should not forget that a strong key person relationship gives the adult a sense of responsibility and a stake in the child's future. Working closely with a child or group of children and being able to celebrate progress with them and their parents is hugely satisfying.

Reflection points

- How do you audit key person relationships in your setting?

- Are all children active in showing 'seeking' behaviours towards their key persons?

- Does the layout and routine of your setting support younger children's opportunities to spend time with their key person?

- How much time do children spend with their key person and how does this correlate to their developmental needs?

Precise assessment

After relationships, the next point of call has to be a precise assessment of children's communication and language skills. In my experience, many practitioners significantly underestimate the gap between children who will 'fly' through school and those who are at some level of disadvantage. This is because not all settings use information that is age-related when assessing children's progress. There are many free sources of information that are readily available on the internet that settings should make use of. At one click, it is possible to find out that by two years of age most children will be using 50 words, or that by three years of age, most of what children say should now be recognisable. The milestones of development on which such information is based have been carefully researched. When this information has been used, practitioners are often more confident and precise in their assessments.

Age-related assessment means that children are referred to speech and language services more promptly, as practitioners are able to recognise the difference between typical and atypical language development. Most speech and language teams have produced leaflets to help

Reflection points

- What sources of information are used to make assessments in your setting?

- Are they age-related?

- Does everyone have a good understanding of typical language development for the age range that they work with?

- How is children's progress tracked?

- How often are summative assessments carried out?

- Do summative assessments indicate progress in relation to expected development?

early years settings understand when they should refer children. At the end of this chapter, you will find the normative development charts that Kent Community Health NHS Foundation Trust have kindly allowed me to reproduce. (See page 105)

Listening carefully to what children say can help with precise assessment.

Summer-born children – a race against time?

In England it is expected that children's language is fluent when they start reception, and are therefore able to learn to read and write. For children who have not mastered language at the start of reception this approach does not necessarily work and the outcomes are worrying. This is reflected by the statistics produced both at the end of the reception and throughout children's school career.

Most children start reception when they are four-years-old. Only a few schools stagger entry and fewer still wait until Year 1 to begin the process of reading. As the milestone for children to reach fluency is four-years-old, this means that the dice are stacked against children born in the summer. A child born in July has just a one month 'margin of error' in terms of reaching fluency and therefore being ready to cope with the reading programme. A six month delay that is picked up and worked on in a child born in September is not likely to be problematic, but this is not true if the child is born in August. Precise assessment and strong interactions are needed for all children, but there is a case to be made for focussing particularly on this group of children. In recent years there has been an increasing focus on the provision for summer-born children. The Department of Education has issued guidance for local authorities and schools stating that parents, if they wish, can request a deferred entry into the reception class. Whereas previously some schools did this on a discretionary basis, the drawback was that children then had to be put back into their 'birth age' cohort, so take up was low. This guidance allows children to stay with the cohort that they joined in reception as they progress through the school, thus making them the oldest children in the class.

- Is tracking for progress made with reference to when a child is due to start reception?

- Are summer born children targeted for more interactions?

- Does your setting help parents know that they can request a deferment so that their child starts reception after they have turned five?

Factors affecting children's communication and language

There are many factors that can increase or reduce children's opportunities to develop communication and language skills. In order to effectively support children's communication and language we need to take these into account.

Background noise

In the chapter on rich play environments, I looked specifically at background noise. (See Chapter 2, page 35.) This is a significant factor that can impact on children's language and speech. Young children, particularly under three-year-olds, really benefit from quieter environments where they can hear speech sounds clearly and can also make their voices heard. Busy environments can also cause problems with children's ability to pay attention; ongoing activity around makes it hard for children to focus on who is speaking, which could be an adult or another child.

Creating small spaces can cut down background noise.

Reflection points

- Do you have quiet rooms or areas indoors?

- How are you creating spaces where children can play, communicate and talk without becoming distracted?

- Which areas in your setting work best for communication and language?

Dummies

One of the factors that can impact on children's communication, language and clear speech is the use of dummies. Overuse of dummies can have the following effects:

- Less facial expression can be shown by the child. This changes the style and length of interactions with others as the child may appear less responsive and positive

- Reduced vocalisations and interactions because talking with the dummy in place is harder. Removing the dummy from the mouth to talk also requires effort

- Unclear speech if children become used to forming sounds with the dummy in their mouth. This means that the tongue cannot reach the teeth

- Greater likelihood of ear infections.

Over the past few years, you may have seen an increase in their use by parents. This is probably because dummies are recommended for sleeping babies in the first year of life in order to reduce the risk of cot death. Whilst the guidance around reducing cot death recommends that they are needed for sleep and only until 12 months, children do become used to having them as comforters. It is important to develop a no dummy policy whilst children are with you, but this does need to be implemented sensitively. A two-year-old who is new to the setting and just finding their feet, does not need the added trauma of having their comforter removed!

It is also important to work with parents so that, over time, their child can manage in the home without a dummy. This is sensitive work and it may be that a step-by-step approach whereby parents set out their own small targets will be the best way forward, e.g. that they will wait ten minutes after the session before giving their child the dummy.

Dummies can prevent children from talking and learning to form speech sounds.

Hearing loss

In early childhood, children are very prone to a build up of fluid in the tube leading from the outer ear to the eardrum. This can be associated with frequent colds and ear infections. It is important to recognise when children are not hearing fully as the impact on their communication and language can be significant. For example:

- Speech is likely to be unclear and difficult to understand because children cannot hear the sounds in words clearly

- Difficulty in responding appropriately as children may not fully hear what has been asked of them or what has been said

- Lack of engagement as some children who are not fully hearing tend to withdraw.

This type of hearing loss can be difficult to detect unless you are actively looking for it. It is an intermittent loss, which means that some weeks children will hear more clearly than others. When talking to parents it is worth stressing that this type of hearing loss is not permanent and outcomes for children are very good if treatment is followed. Any of the following signs may be indicators that a child is not fully hearing and are worth following up:

- Unclear or muffled sounding speech which is hard to understand and not age-appropriate

- Talks loudly and speech may be quite monotone

- Turns devices up to full volume, e.g. computers, television

- Child is not always responsive or seems 'dreamy' or 'in their own world'

- Stares at speaker's face with great concentration (the child may be lip reading)

- Seems to be startled or surprised, e.g. has not noticed that others are tidying up

- Outbursts of frustration.

Reflection points

- Does everyone in the setting know some of the signs that indicate a child may not be hearing fully?

- Do you actively look out for children who may not be hearing fully?

Temperament

Children's temperaments can change according to language and development and can affect their communication and language. Two of the five personality traits identified by researchers as the 'Big five' are particularly worth taking into consideration. Firstly, you should think about children's level of extroversion. How interested and comfortable are they with others? Do they prefer their own company or to be just with one other child or adult? Children who are extrovert are often quick to seek out the company of others and are keen for attention and hence are likely to regularly communicate and interact. On the other hand, a child who is more introverted may prefer to play alone or may not enjoy being part of a group.

The second most important personality trait to consider is openness or curiosity. This is about how interested children are in trying out new things or being open to new experiences. As we have seen in Chapter 4, seeing new things and being open to different experiences may help prompt children's interactions. Being aware of these traits can mean that we are more sensitive in the way that we plan and organise environments and activities. When children are introvert or lack curiousity, it is important not to see this as a problem or something that needs fixing. Instead, see it as yet another example of diversity in action.

Reflection points

- How do you work with parents to find out more about a child's temperament when they join the setting?

- Do you consider children's temperaments when planning activities and experiences?

- How do interactions with children take into consideration their temperaments?

Children's temperament can impact on how often they choose to talk.

The small size of this group allows the children to contribute.

Grouping

One of the challenges when working with mixed aged groups or with children who are at different stages of language development, is how to meet their individual needs. Whilst children who are still in the early stages of language can benefit from being with children who can model language well, there are some drawbacks too.

Processing speeds
Children who have different language levels will process information and language at different speeds. Children whose language is nearly fluent will often anticipate the end of a question or be quicker to articulate a response. The difference in processing speeds often means that children who have the greatest language needs may not have as many opportunities to contribute as children with more developed language.

Language style of adults
Adults working with children should aim to adapt their language style to meet the language level of the child. When children are in mixed language groups, it is much harder for adults to do this and may mean that they pitch their language too high for some children to access.

Small groups for adult-led activities
For children who have language delay, it is important that they are in very small groups. This often means a maximum of three or four in a group. This is because they can find it harder to be attentive and listen when they are in larger groups because they need high levels of eye contact and direct adult involvement. Without a high level of adult involvement, they are unlikely to benefit from the interaction. Participative activities such as dancing to music, rhyme and songs however are exceptions to this.

> ### Reflection points
>
> ● When do you work with children in small groups in your setting?
>
> ● How are these groups organised?
>
> ● How are you monitoring that children with language needs are attending and fully engaged?

Role of the adult

There have been many excellent programmes over the years that have helped early years practitioners focus on children's communication and language. These have included 'Communication Matters' as well as 'Every Child A Talker'. In addition, organisations such as ICAN (www.ican.org.uk) have produced a range of information packs that are extremely useful. It is not therefore my intention in this chapter to re-invent the wheel, but I think it is worth picking out some key points that are worth reflecting on in respect of the role of the adult.

Agreeing on what is a quality interaction

When looking at the role of the adult it is important to come to some agreement as to what you or your team would define as a 'quality interaction'. The diagram below highlights some features that you might consider as essential in a quality interaction:

Length of interactions

'Lucky' children generally have plenty of opportunities to talk with adults and these are often long in duration. It is therefore important to focus on the length of interactions that children have access to. In this context, I use the term 'interactions' to mean connecting with the child in some way. This may include copying their play movements, modelling language as well as talking. Short bursts of comments or snatched conversations are of course better than nothing, but some children will need interactions that last ten or so minutes in order for them to make significant progress. Increasing the length of interactions with some children may require patience and great sensitivity. Not all children are used to having a lot of adult attention or opportunities to be with adults and therefore the way they respond may come across as reluctance to engage.

It is worth monitoring the length of interactions for a while in the setting and checking whether children with the greatest need are having enough time with adults.

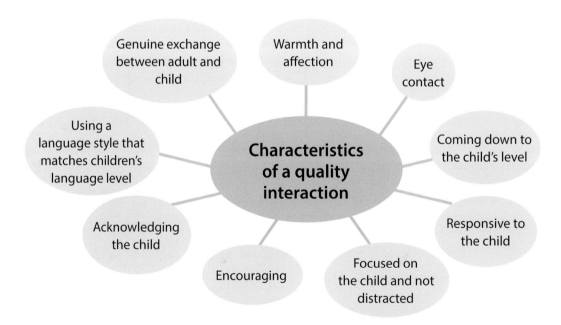

Some activities lend themselves to long interactions with children.

Reflection points

- Do you audit the length of interactions in your setting?

- Have you identified the barriers to lengthy interactions in your setting, e.g. other children and adults interrupting?

- Are the children who are most in need getting lengthy interactions?

- How do you help parents to recognise their role in supporting children's interactions?

Taking a language partner approach

We have seen that relationships play a significant role in supporting communication and language. Some children can make significant gains in their language development if they regularly experience supportive, but naturalistic language opportunities that 'lucky' children have had access to.

The term 'language partner' is one that neatly sums up how adults need to approach interaction with children. A language partner does not specifically 'teach', but instead joins a child in conversation, play and communication. Key features of a language partner approach include the behaviours explored below.

Acknowledgement and encouragement

All communications that children make including gestures, nods or single word utterances should be equally valued. The language partner acknowledges through facial expression as well as words, that the child's attempts at communications are important.

Relaxed situation

The language partner approach should be relaxing and enjoyable for both adults and children. The idea is to allow conversation and communication to develop naturally rather than the adult steering it, so for example if a child's attention is taken by a fly in the room, then that is the topic that is followed!

Space and time to think and talk

Children whose language is still developing need quite a lot of processing time, especially when they are engaging in a new experience. A language partner is able to sense when children need time and so does not continually talk or use questions. They allow for relaxed silences and wait for children to initiate talk.

Modelling

Ofsted evaluations place emphasis on the use of questions as a tool for expanding children's thinking and learning. Whilst for children with good levels of language development this may work well, for children whose language is still developing, there may be other priorities. Children with low levels of language need to hear language being modelled by an adult. They need to hear a full sentence structure and to hear the words in the context associated with the activity. It may be that the starting point when working with some children is to play alongside them, copy their movements and simply narrate what they are doing, e.g. 'The car is going down the tube'.

Language routines

Many children benefit from carrying out regular activities with the same adult. This could be their parent, key person or another adult that they enjoy being with. The activity can be anything from watering a plant, putting plates out for a snack through to sorting out cutlery.

By doing the same thing with the same adult, a language routine develops. The child starts to associate vocabulary and expressions with the activity as the adult models it. After a while, the child can increasingly respond and join in.

Reflection points

- Is a language partner approach taken in your setting?

- Do you ensure that children have sufficient processing time during interactions?

- Does everyone understand the importance of modelling language as well as using sensitive questions?

- Are language routines a significant part of your practice with children who have lower levels of language?

Stimuli

Creating a perfect language environment is a little like a three part jigsaw puzzle. Relationships matter and so does the skill level of the adult. The final part of the jigsaw puzzle is finding something particularly important to talk and communicate about.

It is always interesting to see how some children's interactions with adults and each other increase when they are doing, seeing or touching something new. There are many ways of creating stimuli and one of these is, of course, through providing children with new experiences of the type that we looked at in Chapter 4, (page 61). The need for new stimuli is one reason why the play environment needs to evolve so that children are finding new challenges and resources and hence new things to communicate about. Books are also another strong stimulus and we look at their importance for communication

and language and literacy in Chapter 8 (page 132). Not all stimuli for language can be planned. Sometimes a stimulus for language arises spontaneously and these opportunities need to be grabbed, e.g. a helicopter hovering overhead, a change in the weather or the toast burning – these are all likely to elicit comments.

> ## Reflection points
>
> - Do you provide an environment that encourages interaction?
>
> - Are there new things for children to notice and so talk about?
>
> - Do you follow up on naturally-occurring stimuli that children are interested in?

Relationships

Adult's skill level

Something to talk and communicate about

Monitoring levels of interaction with individual children

We know that for some children who come into our setting the missing ingredient in their lives is adult attention and interaction in their home environment and the emotional and language deficit that this brings with it. Some of the statistics that we looked at from ICAN in the Introduction (See page 8) clearly showed that children at risk of educational disadvantage often had less opportunities for interaction than their 'lucky' counterparts. This is one of the reasons why their vocabulary levels can be lower as well as their language levels. Although children can pick up some language just by playing with other children, this in itself is unlikely to be sufficient. It is therefore sensible to monitor that individual children are getting the levels of interaction with adults that they need.

If you are working as a childminder, the chances are that unless there are exceptional circumstances you are not likely to have more than three children under five with you at any one time. This guarantees that children will have plenty of opportunities for frequent and sustained interaction. If, on the other hand, you are working in a busy group setting where there are several adults and also a lot of space, knowing how much interaction a child has had becomes a little trickier. It is easy to assume that the other adults have played with the child or engaged in meaningful language-rich activities, such as sharing a book.

A good starting point is therefore to create a very simple monitoring sheet that keeps a record of the number of interactions that have taken place in a session with the children that need more language support. For the purpose of this chart, I would argue that only interactions that last more than five minutes should be included as we know that brief interactions are less effective. You could also create a code to show where there have been extended interactions of say ten minutes or more that have taken place. It may also be worth initialling which staff member has interacted with the child.

Name of child	Monday	Tuesday	Wednesday	Thursday	Friday
Ayse	✓ ✓ ✓ PT AM PT ✓ ✓ PT PT				
Taylor	✓ JM				
Tia	✓ ✓ ✓ AT PT PT				
Josh	✓ ✓ JM AT				

Some children will need to be targeted for additional interactions by adults.

How to use the monitoring sheet

We know that to make progress some children will need plenty of quality interactions during the session. The sheet can therefore be used initially to assess the number of quality interactions that are actually taking place. As a result of the initial tracking, as a team, you will need to think about whether individual children are having sufficient interactions and whether going forward, you will need to target individual children for more interactions.

Reflection points

- How do you monitor levels of interaction that individual children are getting?

- Do you need to target children for increased interactions?

How many interactions

There is no magic number of interactions associated with language acquisition. My personal feeling is that you should consider what 'lucky children' would be getting if they were with a supportive parent. This is particularly important when you look at two-year-olds, as many parents of this age group would say that over a three-hour period, interactions are pretty constant. As a team, or alone if you are a childminder, it is worth thinking about what you feel a child should be getting, given their age and level of development and then comparing this to the actual number of interactions that are taking place.

Targeting children

In some settings, the level of need is very significant. You may therefore decide to take some advice about how best to organise your provision and targeting. It may be, for example, that you decide to focus on some children for a set duration, e.g. two weeks. Ideally, it will be worth making sure that parents know that you are having a 'language push' so that they can also focus on interactions at home.

Specific skills to support children's communication and language development

There are several areas that we can work on with children in order to further support their communication and language. These are often areas of weakness amongst children who are at risk of education disadvantage. Working closely on these may therefore help to close the attainment gap later on.

Listening and attention

Listening and attention is the cornerstone of language learning and so is an area to focus on with some children. To do this effectively, you will need to assess how easy these children find it to focus on a speaker. In terms of typical development, for example, most children aged two will find it hard to concentrate on a speaker while they are engaged in other interesting activities. Listening and attention skills are linked to children's acquisition of speech sounds as well as developing their phonological awareness that is key for early literacy. (See also Chapter 8, page 132)

A good starting point to support children's listening skills is to make sure that we model active listening. This means making sure that children get our full attention and eye contact when they are trying to communicate with us. For some children, this can be the missing link as they may not have seen how to listen before. When there are groups of children competing for our attention, being an active listener can be tricky, but we do need to make sure that children

Games to support listening

Name recognition games	Examples:
	• Run around the circle when you hear your name
	• Clap your hands when you hear your name
	• Put a brick in the cardboard tube when you hear your name.
Musical games that promote listening	Examples
	• Stop and start
	• Musical statues
	• 'Simon Says…'
Traditional games changed to involve sounds	Examples:
	• Hunt the thimble – but instead of saying hot or cold, children use the volume of shakers to know if they are getting closer.

who need this from us are prioritised in some way. It is also helpful to create an environment that helps children be attentive. Background noise and environments where there is a lot of movement can be distracting for young children. It is therefore helpful to create some spaces that are quiet and 'still' in which activities that can support listening and attention can be carried out for those children who need this. There are many activities that can support listening including those on page 102. In addition, you might like to try some of the games below which are simpler to start with – especially those games involving children listening out for their name.

Reflection points

- Do you model active listening skills so that children can see how to listen?

- How do you work with parents to increase the number of active listening opportunities for children?

- Do you plan specific listening activities to help children who need to develop these skills?

Turn-taking

Some children talk well, but are not so good at turn-taking. It is a skill that is needed not just in communication, but it is also a key social skill, as we saw in the previous chapter (see page 77). Taking turns needs to be modelled for children and so it is important that we look for opportunities to model this skill by not interrupting them, for example.

As this is partly a developmental skill, we also need to be mindful of situations that will be particularly difficult for children. These include large group situations and when a situation is very stimulating or exciting. In such situations, it will be hard for children not to call out or interrupt others as their brains are in 'overload' mode. Interestingly, thinking aloud, known as 'external speech' is a feature of young children's development. It is one reason why children often make continual comments during story sessions and find it so hard not to 'blurt out' answers when in groups. For most children, thinking and talking aloud persists until they have mastered language and can internalise their thinking.

Speech

Being able to produce speech sounds is a developmental process that depends on several factors. These include muscles in the tongue and position of the teeth, as well as children being able to hear and focus on speech clearly in order to reproduce it.

It is important to recognise when children's speech production is not typical for their age as this can result in them becoming frustrated because others cannot understand them and therefore their attempts at communication may decrease. (At the end of this chapter, there is a chart that shows typical age-related progression in speech sounds, see page 107).

We can support children's speech by talking clearly, not using harsh tones or raising our voices and trying to use tuneful voices. Cutting down background noise is also helpful. In terms of specific activities, the use of listening games can help children as can having a nursery rhyme programme. (See also Chapter 4, page 65)

Reflection points

- Do you monitor background noise in your setting?

- How do you ensure that your voice tones with children are conducive to supporting speech?

- Do you regularly say and use nursery rhymes?

Vocabulary

Some children may be talking regularly, but may still need opportunities to develop vocabulary. Children learn vocabulary in context and when it is meaningful in some way for them. Key to vocabulary development is the role of the adult. Whilst children can acquire vocabulary from hearing other children talk, it is principally something that adults need to take responsibility for. We have seen already how experiences can develop children's vocabulary, but there are many other stimuli including role play, games such as picture lotto and books.

It can be worth taking a strategic approach to building children's vocabulary through the use of long-term planning. There are many ways of doing this, and this may include starting with the experiences, role play and activities that you believe children will enjoy and benefit from and then being aware of the associated vocabulary.

You could also take another tack. You could think about the areas of vocabulary for which children need support and then look for books, activities and resources that would support them. Whatever you decide, it is important that you check that children have sufficient functional vocabulary so that they can express themselves on a day-to-day basis, e.g. about feelings, clothes and food.

Reflection points

- How do you assess children's vocabulary?

- Do you plan strategically to expand children's vocabulary?

- How do you organise resources to help children develop new vocabulary?

Summary

In the introduction to the book we saw that language levels are one of the areas on which we must carefully focus if we are to actively help children who are at risk of disadvantage. In this chapter we have seen the links between language and cognition and how it underpins learning to read and write. In this chapter I have focused on the importance of precise assessment, and one of the things that you might like to look at are the normative development charts that have been included here. You may also like to think carefully about the quality, length and frequency of interactions in your setting and whether children who need them most are indeed benefitting from them.

Development of Comprehension (Understanding) Developmental Norm Chart

Age	Would usually have/use	Concerns if	Don't worry if
1.6 – 1.11	• Understands basic everyday instructions e.g. where is your shoe /show me your nose • Knows and turns to own name	• Child struggles to follow basic instructions • Does not turn to own name • Also refer to risk factors	• Child does not understand complex instructions • Does not know colours/numbers • Cannot respond to questions
	At this stage (1;6 -1;11) monitor progress and provide general language and play advice and signpost to Children's Centres		
2.0 – 2.5	• Understands single words and most simple two word commands (objects and actions) • Understands questions such as what/where/who • Understands basic concepts such as big/little	• Does no respond to what/where questions (responses can be verbal/non verbal • Understanding at a one to two word level • Also refer to risk factors	• Child struggles to follow some longer complex instructions with abstract concepts • Does not know their colours/numbers • If they do not understand more complex vocabulary • Cannot respond to "why" questions
2.06 – 2.11	• Understands more complex instructions (2-3 word level) • Follows routines well • Understands words such as 'wet', 'dry', 'big' and 'little' • Understands simple stories • Listens with interest when spoken to	• Vague look when asked a simple question • Always follows what others are doing • Shows little interest in what is happening around them • Responses are not what you would expect e.g. "Where's mummy?" child responds "Jack"	• Child struggles to follow some longer complex instructions • Does not know their colours/numbers • If they do not understand more complex vocabulary • Cannot respond to "why" questions
3.00 – 3.05	• Begins to understand the word 'not' • Can start to identify objects in categories (e.g. can you find me the animals) • Understand simple stories	• Any of the above • Child does not understand a simple story • Appears to only understand if shown what you mean in pictures/gestures • Finds it difficult to cope with change • You need to repeat yourself a lot • You need to break instructions down	• Does not know their colours/numbers • If they do not understand more complex vocabulary • Cannot respond to "why" questions • Child is unable to easily follow an adult conversation but does try
3.06 – 3.11	• Answers questions such as "how did you get here?" • Understands opposites • Beginning to understand the concept of time • Follows requests of several parts	• Any of the above • Only seems to understand naming words • Finding it difficult to interact with peers; play tends to be more physical than imaginative	• Does not know their colours/numbers • If they do not understand more complex vocabulary • Cannot respond to "why" questions • Child is unable to easily follow an adult conversation but does try
4.00 – 5.00	• Follows adult conversation • Understands many time concepts • Follows conversations which may include the past or future	• Any of the above • Child talks in long sentences but it doesn't seem related to the topic	• Does not know their colours/numbers • If they do not understand more complex vocabulary • Child is unable to easily follow an adult conversation but does try

Speech Sound Development Developmental Norm Chart

Age	Would usually have	Refer if	Don't worry if
2.00 – 2.05	m, p, t, d, n, w	• Do not refer for speech sounds only at this age	• Child's speech cannot be understood by unfamiliar people as this is normal at this stage
2.06 – 2.11	m, p, b, t, d, n, w, f, s, h	• Limited range of sounds e.g. only uses 'd' • Vowels are wrong e.g. bee→ bar • Says 't' and 'd' as 'k' and 'g', e.g. tea → key, door → goor • Child dribbles a lot, and has sluggish tongue movements or chewing difficulties • Unable to copy early single sounds, e.g. 'p', 'b', 'm', 'n', 't', 'd' • Uses unusual sounds not typically heard in the English language • Child talks through their nose • No-one, including parents understand the child (even in 1:1 situation in a quiet environment or when context known)	• Speech is not always clear • Misses off endings of words e.g. tap → ta • Says 'p', 't' and 'k' as 'b', 'd' and 'g', e.g. pie → bye, toe → doe, car → gar • Says 'f' as 'p' and 'b', e.g. four → bour • Says 's' as 't' or 'd', e.g. sun → dun • Says 'k' and 'g' as 't' and 'd', e.g. car → tar, girl → dirl • Reduces two consonants together in a word to one consonant, e.g. star → tar, spider → pider • Says 'sh', 'ch' and 'j' as 's', 't' and 'd', e.g. sheep → seep, cheese → teese, jelly → delly • Confuses 'l', 'y' 'w', and 'r', yellow → lellow, red → wed • Finds 'l' and 'r' blends difficult, e.g. blue → bu, train → rain • 's' produced between the teeth, e.g. bus → buth (lisps) • Says 'th' as 'd', 'f' or 'v', e.g. think → fink
3.00 – 3.05	m, p, b, t, d, n, w, f, s, y, h, ng, k, g, l, s, z, v	• Any of the above • Missing off the beginnings of words e.g. pig →ig	• Speech is not 100 % clear • Misses off endings of words e.g. tap → ta • Says 'p', 't' and 'k' as 'b', 'd' and 'g', e.g. pie → bye, toe → doe, car → gar • Says 'f' as 'p' and 'b', e.g. four → bour • Says 's' as 't' or 'd', e.g. sun → dun • Says 'k' and 'g' as 't' and 'd', e.g. car → tar, girl → dirl • Reduces two consonants together in a word to one consonant, e.g. smoke → moke, spider → bider • Says 'p', 't' and 'k' as 'b', 'd' and 'g' e.g. pie → bye, toe → doe, car → gar • Says 'sh', 'ch' and 'j' as 's', 't' and 'd', e.g. sheep → seep, cheese → teese, jelly → delly • Confuses 'l', 'y', 'w', and 'r', yellow → lellow, red → wed • Finds 'l' and 'r' blends difficult, e.g. blue → bu, train → rain • 's' produced between the teeth, e.g. bus → buth (lisps) • Says 'th' as 'd', 'f' or 'v', e.g. think → fink

Age	Would usually have	Refer if	Don't worry if
3.06 – 3.11	m, p, b, t, d, n, w, f, s, y, h, ng, k, g, l, s, z, v	• Any of the above • Has very few sounds and inconsistent, different productions of the same words • In a 1:1 situation in a quiet environment or when context known most familiar people still have difficulty understanding child	• Speech is not 100 % clear • Says 'k' and 'g' as 't' and 'd', e.g. car → tar, girl → dirl • Reduces two consonants together in a word to one consonant, e.g. star → tar, spider → pider • Says 'sh', 'ch' and 'j' as 's', 't' and 'd', e.g. sheep → seep, cheese → teese, jelly → delly • Says 'f' as 'p' and 'b', e.g. four → bour • Confuses 'l', 'y', 'w', and 'r', yellow → lellow, red → wed • Finds 'l' and 'r' blends difficult, e.g. blue → bu, train → rain • 's' produced between the teeth, e.g. bus → buth (lisps) • Says 'th' as 'd', 'f' or 'v', e.g. think → fink
4.00 – 4.05	All of the above + ch, j	• Any of the above	• Speech is not 100 % clear • Reduces two consonants together in a word to one consonant, e.g. star → tar, spider → pider • Says 'sh', 'ch' and 'j' as 's', 't' and 'd', e.g. sheep → seep, cheese → teese, jelly → delly • Says 'k' and 'g' as 't' and 'd', e.g. car → dar, girl → dirl • Confuses 'l' 'y', 'w', and 'r', yellow → lellow, red → wed • Finds 'l' and 'r' blends difficult, e.g. blue → bu, train → rain • 's' produced between the teeth, e.g. bus → buth (lisps) • Says 'th' as 'd', 'f' or 'v', e.g. think → fink
4.06 – 5.05	Most sounds in isolation are clear and easy to understand	• Any of the above	• Reduces two consonants together in a word to one consonant, e.g. star → tar, spider → pider • Confuses 'l', 'y', 'w', and 'r', yellow → lellow, red → wed • Finds 'l' and 'r' blends difficult, e.g. blue → bu, train → rain • 's' produced between the teeth, e.g. bus → buth • Says 'th' as 'd', 'f' or 'v', e.g. think → fink • Says 'sh', 'ch' and 'j' as 's', 't' and 'd', e.g. sheep → seep, cheese → teese, jelly → delly
5.06 – 6.06	Generally clear and easy to understand	• Any of the above	• Confuses 'l', 'y', 'w', and 'r', yellow → lellow, red → wed • Finds 'l' and 'r' blends difficult, e.g. blue → bu, train → rain • Says 'th' as 'd', 'f' or 'v', e.g. think → fink • 's' produced between the teeth, e.g. bus → buth

Development of Expression (Use of language) Developmental Norm Chart

Age	Would usually have/use	Concerns if	Don't worry if
1.6 – 1.11	• Minimum of 25 words • Desire to communicate both verbally and non verbally • Attempting to copy sounds and words	• No desire to communicate • Only 5 - 10 words • See risk factors opposite	• Child's words are not completely clear • Baby talk is still used for some words
	At this stage (1.6 -1.11) monitor progress and provide general language and play advice and signpost to Children's Centres		
2.0 – 2.06	• Using a minimum of 50 words and some two word combinations • Using early action words • Shows and names body parts	• Less than 50 words reported • No attempt to join words • 3 or more relevant risk factors	• Sounds are still unclear • Continues to use some baby talk
2.06 – 2.11	• Has approximately 300 words • Asks simple questions • Is linking words together • Using action words • Stammering common • Describes what an object is for • Using own name • Using adjectives/position words	• Child makes no attempt to interact/communicate • Child's vocabulary is not increasing • Child is not beginning to join words e.g. 'more juice'	• Lots of sounds are still unclear • Child is beginning to join words • Child uses baby talk for some words e.g. bikki for biscuit • Child misses out little words in sentences e.g. a/the/tense endings
3.00 – 3.05	• Sentences of 4+ words in length • Good vocabulary • Simple story/event telling • Having conversations • Asks lots of questions	• Any of the above • Child does not use everyday words e.g. cup, car • Child is not using any action words • Child echoes sentences	• Child can be a little shy with strangers • Child still has some speech difficulties • Child misses off/confuses verb tense endings
3.06 – 3.11	• Sentences of 5 - 6 words in length • Knows wide range of vocabulary • Starting to describe past/present experiences • Completes analogies	• Sentences are very short • Child uses non specific words a lot e.g. 'it'/'there'/'do' • Child is not communicating with others • Not having a conversation	• Still has some speech difficulties (see speech sheet) • Makes grammatical errors e.g. "I runned to the shop"
4.00 – 5.00	• Sentences of 6 -8 words in length • Knows wide range of vocabulary • Uses full sentences with the words in the right order • Speaks of imaginary conditions • Uses joining words e.g. and	• Any of the above • Child misses out most grammatical markers • Child cannot tell a simple story • Child cannot talk about the past and future	• Makes mild grammatical errors • Confuses he/she/him/her

For children under the age of 2 ½ years please indicate any risk factors*

In view of recent research on late talkers, take into consideration the following risk factors;

- quiet as an infant/limited babbling
- family history of communication delay
- recurrent ear infections
- limited consonant repertoire
- lack of sequenced pretend play
- mild delay in receptive skills
- lack of, or reduced use of, communicative gestures

- lack of verbal imitation
- limited vocabulary consisting of mostly nouns and few or no verbs
- poor social skills (difficulty initiating and participating with peers
- limited change over time
- Three or more risk factors are significant.

*Olswang, Rodriguez & Timler (1998): Recommending Intervention for Toddlers With Specific Language Difficulties: We May Not Have the Answers, But We Know a Lot" American Journal of Speech-Language Pathology, 23-32.

Chapter 7

Supporting bilingual children

Statistics show that bilingual children often underperform. Therefore, when addressing ways of closing the gap, we must include strategies to work more effectively with this group of children.

One of the significant changes to have occurred in the past fifteen or so years, is the number of children who have access to a language other than English. My own children fall into this category, as we are a bilingual family. There are now very few early years settings that consist only of monolingual children and so it is essential that we understand how best to support children who are learning English from scratch or have limited English. For some children, their risk of disadvantage is increased by the myths that surround bilingualism, and the lack of knowledge about how to support English alongside a home language. This can result in children not always gaining the support they need to become fluent on entry into reception which in turn impacts on their opportunity to learn to read and write.

In this chapter, I begin by giving a background to bilingualism because developing a good understanding is key to good practice. In addition, I want to consider how we can best support and assess the differing needs of children who are either new to English or who are learning it alongside another language. I also want to consider the advice and information that we provide for parents so that they can make informed decisions about their language use at home.

What is bilingualism?

For the purpose of this chapter, the term 'bilingual' is used to mean that a child has access to one or more languages on a daily or regular basis in addition to English. As this book is primarily focused on children aged five years and under, definitions about the level of fluency are not so relevant, as some children will not be fluent in any language although their progress will be age-appropriate.

How children may acquire more than one language

One of the most important things to understand when looking at bilingualism is that children will develop English very differently. It is a huge mistake therefore to make any assumptions about the needs of individual children without understanding the context in which they are learning languages.

Simultaneous (home language alongside English from a very young age)

For some children, their home language and English are learnt alongside each other. There are a number of ways in which this might occur. It may that one parent speaks English to their child while the other uses their home language. For other children, it may be that although their parents speak to them in their home language, they have had a lot of exposure to English since they were born. This might be because they live and interact within a community where English is predominantly spoken. English has therefore always been part of their lives, even though it has only been learnt through interactions with carers and/or family friends or during parent and toddler groups.

Sequential (English is learnt after the home language is established)

An increasing number of early years settings are likely to take in children who have had no previous exposure or very limited exposure to English. It is helpful to see these children as 'new to English' rather than having English as an 'additional language', because the reality is, at this point, they have not yet acquired English. There are many reasons why children may learn English sequentially. For some children, their parents have moved to the United Kingdom to seek work, to take up a role or as refugees. There will also be some children who learn English sequentially who have always lived in the United Kingdom. They may have had little or no exposure to English because they live and interact in a community where English is not the predominant language.

> ## Reflection points
>
> - Does everyone in your setting understand that there are two ways in which children may acquire more than one language?
>
> - Is a note made in their records of the way that children are acquiring languages?

Many children have both English and another home language.

Myths

A good starting point is to explore some of the myths that surround bilingualism, as some of these can be very misleading and can be linked to poor practice.

Myth 1

Children who can use more than one language are clever

Whilst there are some cognitive gains, the reality is that children who have the opportunity to learn more than one language are simply lucky. Assuming typical development, any child has the capacity to learn more than one language providing they have sufficient exposure and interactions.

Myth 2

Babies and toddlers learning more than one language may become confused

Although it is helpful if each language that the child is learning is used with some consistency, children are born with the innate skill of detecting patterns and structures of language. Having the opportunity to learn two languages side by side does not cause any particular problems.

Myth 3

Children who are learning English simultaneously alongside a home language are likely to be delayed in their language acquisition

The production of first words can be a little later in toddlers, however this not necessarily always the case. Having said this, when there is a language delay, it does need to be investigated as there may be other underlying reasons that are causing the delay.

Myth 4

Children whose parents speak another language will automatically gain fluency in the parental language

There is an assumption that children whose parents speak a language other than English will automatically pick up their parents' language. This is not always the case. It will depend on how much exposure and thus time parents are spending using their language with the child. When parents use English rather than their home language, they may not have sufficient exposure for children to become fluent users.

Myth 5

Children who come into a setting without English will soon pick it up from playing with the other children

Whilst playing and interacting with other children will be helpful, this in itself is not likely to be sufficient for children to make speedy progress. Sequential learners need a lot of sensitive support from adults in order to maximise the rate at which they acquire English.

Myth 6

It is best that children learn English first and then later on learn their home language

This approach can be ineffective, as many parents learn to their cost! Once English is established, it can be very hard for parents to introduce their home language afterwards. In addition, when children are not learning their home language they are, in effect, being denied opportunities to develop their cultural and self-identity. (See 'Importance of bilingualism', page 114)

Myth 7

A bilingual child can have a language disorder in one language but not the other

Where children have a language disorder, it will appear in both languages. This is why it is important to understand how well the child is progressing in the home language, especially when there are any difficulties with the child's English.

Reflection points

- How do you ensure that everyone in your setting is knowledgeable about bilingual children?

- Do you challenge these myths when you hear them?

How young children learn more than one language

Languages are in effect codes that children have to identify, break into and then learn to use. Every spoken language has universal constituent parts:

- Phonology – the sounds that are needed to produce the words in the language

- Vocabulary – the words of the language

- Grammar – how the words are put together to form sentences including questions

- Semantics – understanding the meanings of words and phrases including idioms such as 'it's raining cats and dogs'

- Pragmatics – how and when to use the language.

For children who are learning more than one language, they will need to learn how each code works. Although some languages are similar in their grammar, others operate very differently, e.g. in English we use prepositions such as 'on the table', whilst in other languages such as Turkish, postpositions are used, e.g. 'masada' (masa = table, da=on).

Regardless of whether children learn languages simultaneously or sequentially, the way in which they pick them up remains the same as for monolingual children. Children learn languages through interactions with others and exposure in their immediate environment. It is an active rather than passive process; humans have an innate ability to 'crack the code' of whatever language is presented, thus no one language is harder than any other for young children. Having said this, the level of contact and exposure that children have with each language will determine how quickly it is acquired and whether fluency is gained.

Unequal levels of proficiency

Very few bilingual children or adults gain equal levels of proficiency across both or all of the languages, although many will be fluent users. This is because, as we have seen in Chapter 6, page 86), language learning is linked to both exposure and context. In particular, exposure is very important as to whether two languages are both acquired with equal proficiency, e.g.

Not all bilingual children will have the opportunity to become literate in their home language.

that children master all elements of each of the languages available to them. Where exposure to a language is very low, children are likely to be able to acquire receptive language whereby they can listen and understand, but they may not be able to talk fluently in that language. This is sometimes referred to as 'passive bilingualism'.

Even when older children and adults are fluent in different languages, it is likely when it comes to particular functions such as mathematics, that they will favour carrying out the problem solving and calculations in the language in which they were taught and rehearsed the skill. In addition, children and adults will also have pockets of different vocabulary that has been acquired through context and so it is not unusual for a child to know the word for 'sofa' in their home language, but not in English. This can result in code switching, whereby one word from the language is substituted into a sentence because its equivalent is not known.

Some children will become literate in their home language if they are given specific instruction, but this is not an automatic process. This means that some bilingual children will always be more comfortable reading and writing in English as they have had more exposure and instruction in this language. Interestingly, when children have access to bilingual systems of education where instruction is given in both languages, this may be less of an issue.

The importance and benefits of bilingualism

Language is above all a social code that allows us to connect with other people. Relationships are formed and reinforced through the medium of language as well as through non-verbal communication. This means that for many children the principle benefit of being bilingual is that it allows them to understand, communicate and enjoy, not just their immediate family, but also their extended family, community and culture. Through language, children's self-identity is developed as well as an understanding and sense of belonging to the community of same language users.

Interestingly, bilingualism also seems to have a positive impact on children's cognition. There have been several pieces of research that show that bilingual children are able to focus their attention more easily than monolingual children. In a task known as the 'Shape stroop test', toddlers were shown pictures of a large fruit that had a smaller different fruit inside it, e.g. a banana inside an apple. Children were asked to point to the smaller fruit, i.e. the banana. Typically, most monolingual children would point to the large fruit as it is more obvious, whilst bilingual children were able to correctly follow the instruction.

In addition, bilingual children also seem to find it easier to switch their attention between tasks and so may have more cognitive flexibility. And finally, there have also been studies to show that in later life the onset of dementia seems to be delayed amongst lifelong bilinguals.

So, all in all, bilingualism is good news for children!

A bilingual child might find it easier to complete two jigsaw puzzles at the same time than a monolingual child.

Supportive environments

In theory there are many benefits of bilingualism, however this depends on whether or not children and their parents are in supportive environments. Although all early years settings and schools are required to have an equality and diversity policy that will focus on anti-discrimination, the reality is that some adults within early years settings and schools still find bilingualism a huge inconvenience. This is usually because they are monolingual and so have little understanding of the importance of bilingualism. They may also have the misguided notion that to successfully learn English, the home language needs to be jettisoned. This approach is sometimes referred to as 'subtractive bilingualism'.

In supportive environments, there is an understanding of the importance of the home language and the benefits that it brings. Indeed bilingualism is celebrated at every opportunity. This approach is sometimes referred to as 'additive bilingualism'. Research shows that it is this approach that is the most effective and will support children's positive achievement.

There are many ways of creating supportive environments for bilingual children and families. They begin with physically valuing the child's home language and culture by, for example, having a welcome sign and taking time to correctly learn to pronounce both the child's and the parents' names. Other physical indicators may include fabrics, props and pictures that accurately represent the family's culture. A supportive environment will also include some books in the child's home language and, since we all now have technology, some resources where the child can see/hear their home language, e.g. a game on a tablet.

For children who are totally new to English or have only recently started learning it, it is also helpful for them to have spaces where they can 'retreat' and where they are able to play without having to focus on English.

Starting out – learning about language use at home

The starting point in helping both simultaneous and new to English bilingual children is to learn as much as you can about the way that language is used at home. It is important not to make any assumptions.

Simultaneous bilinguals

It is particularly important to find out about how much exposure and knowledge the child has of both the home language and English. In some cases, simultaneous bilingual children may have acquired a high level of receptive English, but are not yet actively using it, or the reverse. It is also helpful to find out which person or people speak to the child in the home language and whether this takes place consistently, e.g. some parents talk to their child in the home language at home but when out and about will address their child in English. In some families, it may be that more than one language is being used with the child and it is helpful to know how these are used.

Sequential bilinguals

For children who will be learning English as a new language, you should also talk to their parents and find out about language use at home. When doing this, it is important that parents do not reach the conclusion that they need to stop using the home language and to switch to English. As with simultaneous bilingual children, we do need to find out how well the child is progressing in the home language. This is important as if there is a language delay or disorder, this will impact on children's progress with English. Ideally, if parents cannot self-report about their child's progress, it would be worth using a translator to facilitate this conversation.

Finding out about the family's culture

As well as finding out as much as we can about the child's languages, it is also important that we try to find out about the culture of the family. This is important because we need to understand to what extent there will be significant cultural differences that may become an additional challenge for the child on top of learning a new language. In particular, it is worth finding out about the child's name, including how it is pronounced and if it has a meaning in the home language. It also worth finding out what the expectations of parents are in terms of their child's learning and approach to play. This might include finding out at what age children in their culture usually begin to learn to read and write or have homework. We also need to find out about routines such as mealtimes, toileting and dressing. (See also Chapter 10, page 174)

T!P

Finding out about a child's home language

These questions might be useful when finding out about a child's home language use:

- Does the parent have any concerns about how their child is using the home language?

- How well does the child understand the home language?

- Does the child have any words in the home language?

- Does the child join words together in the home language?

Progress in the home language

Where possible, it is also important to find out the progress so far that their child is making in their home language, although this might not always be possible unless the parent has a good level of English or another speaker can translate for them.

Settling in and the key person role

Whilst it is important that all children are settled in carefully and at their own speed, this is particularly essential for children who are new to English. It is hard to imagine what it must be like for a child to come into an alien environment where suddenly they cannot understand anyone and can't make themselves understood. For parents who speak no English, it must be hard as well to trust a stranger with your child knowing that they have now lost their means of communicating. It is therefore essential that additional time is allowed for the child to develop a strong relationship with their key person before separation takes place, and also that the parent becomes familiar and confident with the setting. The key person will start to be the child's guide and security blanket and it is likely that to start with, the child will not want to be out of sight of their key person. To prevent the child from becoming distressed if this person is not available, once the child has settled in, it will be important if another adult can also develop a strong bond with the child so that the child always has someone that they can count on.

Look out for a wide range of resources to facilitate communication with a child.

Using resources to help settling in

Ideally it would be useful to have an interpreter in these situations. If this is not possible consider using a wide range of resources to help this process, including visual aids such as photographs and also technology such as online dictionaries and google translate which, although not perfect, may be helpful. In addition, there is a range of resources designed to support practitioners with bilingual children which use 'magic pens' that when swiped across an image or sentence will say pre-recorded worded phrases. Of particular use when settling in is a picture dictionary and a chart with basic phrases, e.g. see www.mantralingua.com. It is also possible to buy resources that allow you to record words or phrases next to photographs or pictures. In the settling in period, it can be worth working with parents to build up a useful repertoire of words and phrases linked to objects or actions such as, 'Going to the toilet', which are then recorded.

Adjusting the environment

As a result of finding out about the child's culture as well as home language before children start in your setting, it should be possible to consider the environment and find ways of helping the child and parent to feel a little more reassured. The starting point is, out of courtesy, to learn a greeting in the child's home language. Although it is often recommended to learn several key words, this is not always easy where languages have several different inflections for one word, but even in those languages it is at least possible to learn a single word for a greeting. We can also make the environment feel more familiar by displaying books and posters in the child's home language, putting out some toys that we know are the child's favourites and also by using resources that reflect the colours, textures and sounds of the home. This might include fabrics, role play items or objects such as pottery.

Modelling play and expectations

During the settling in process, it is also worth spending time playing with children in different situations and carefully observing their reactions. Not all children will know how to use the different resources and toys in your setting. By modelling their use and playing with children, you can help reduce children's anxiety about doing the 'wrong thing'. It is also helpful to note whether some children/parents dislike sensory materials or seem concerned about getting messy.

Reflection points

- How flexible is your settling in process to support children who are new to English?

- Do you have resources that will help parents who do not speak English to understand the process?

- How do you ensure that children who do not have English are sufficiently attached to their key person to cope with separation?

- In what ways do you adapt the environment to make it reassuring and familiar for parents and children?

- How do you help children and parents to understand what happens in your setting?

- How do you ensure that the child will be able to communicate with you after their parent leaves, e.g. pictures, recorded words?

- Do you observe how bilingual children play?

- Do you actively model play for bilingual children during the settling in period?

Meeting the needs of simultaneous bilingual children

The needs of children who come into the setting already operating in both languages are slightly different to those of children who will be new to English. Firstly, these children already have some English, although in some cases it may be receptive rather than expressive. This means that settling in can be easier, although children may need to 'acclimatise' to the new culture and expectations of your provision.

Gaps in vocabulary

One of the reasons why some children who are learning English alongside another home language may not fulfil their potential is that they may appear to be developing English very well and, indeed in some cases, adults may not even realise that they have a home language which is different from English. Whilst in terms of grammar and being able to communicate their needs, these children may be doing well, but they often have gaps in their vocabulary development. Typical gaps include words related to tasks and objects used in the home. This usually occurs because children are hearing these words in their home language and have not had opportunities to hear them in English. This means that a child might not know words such as 'teaspoon' or 'stir'. In addition, many children will have acquired the language used in relation to concepts such as time, size, shape and colour in their home language and again may need opportunities to hear and use them in English.

There are many ways of helping children develop vocabulary and so close the potential gaps in their knowledge. Firstly, it requires adults to model language in context and also to name objects and actions accurately. It is also helpful to use books in a strategic way so that children hear words and phrases several times and so become secure. For children who are active role players, ensuring that the role play environment has 'detailed' resources becomes very important as they then act as prompts for vocabulary, e.g. oven gloves, drainer and washing up liquid in the kitchen or a magazine rack in the lounge.

Through role play, bilingual children can learn equivalent vocabulary in English.

Reflection points

- How do you assess bilingual children's progress in gaining vocabulary?

- Do you have a planned approach to helping bilingual children acquire vocabulary, e.g. use of books or picture lotto?

- Are there role play opportunities that will help children to hear and use English vocabulary and so learn 'home' words?

Meeting the needs of sequential learners

For children who will be learning English from scratch, we need to be very sensitive to their emotional needs as well as their linguistic ones. Focusing only on learning English is not likely to be effective since language is learnt through a complex pattern of emotional and social interactions. It is also important to remember that although children may not yet be able to communicate using English, they are still able to communicate in other ways, e.g. gesture, facial expressions and body language. The role of the key person and the settling in process will have a marked impact on children's journey into English. This journey normally consists of four stages. It is helpful if everyone including the child's parents knows about these stages.

Stage 1
Continued use of home language

Stage 2
Non-verbal period

Stage 3
Telegraphic and formulaic language

Stage 4
Productive language

Stage 1

Continued use of home language

In this phase, children keep using their home language because their experience to date has been that communicating using this code is effective. It takes some time for some children, particularly younger ones to realise that this no longer works. This is very disorientating for children and it is important that adults are very warm and nurturing during this period. It is also important not to stop children from trying to use their home language as this may be interpreted by children that they are doing something wrong.

Stage 1: meeting children's needs

- Show that children's attempts at communication are acknowledged through body language, gestures or repeating back in English

- Use warm and nurturing body language so that children know that whilst their language is not being recognised, they are!

- Use photographs, facial expressions, pointing and assistive technology such as magic pens to facilitate communication

- Look for opportunities for children to show their competence, e.g. pouring their own drink

- Look for play opportunities and activities which do not necessarily require high levels of language that allow children to join other children.

Non-verbal period

The non-verbal or 'silent' period is a similar stage that babies pass through as they first begin to 'tune in' to language. I prefer the term 'non-verbal' as this is more positive and reminds us that children are still communicating. The length of time that children will spend in this phase depends on many factors (see below), but also the level of support that they receive. In this period, a child will start to hear patterns and sounds of the language and also the meanings of key words that are relevant to them and have also been repeated. When children are working their way through the non-verbal stage, it is important that they are not left to simply get on with it as, like babies, they need plenty of opportunities for meaningful interactions when they can participate and hear language in context, e.g. helping to put out cups at the snack table. Adults also have to change their language style when working with children and work in ways similar to that used with babies. This includes using simplifying sentences, repeating key words or phrases and also using high levels of facial expression, intonation and gestures, e.g.:

'Look. SAND.' [Adult points at the sand tray]

'Here's the SAND!' [Child touches the sand.]

'In goes the SAND.' [Adult puts some sand in a container]

This style also involves repeating movements whilst repeating phrases. This helps children to learn the words for actions as well as objects. In this phase, you should consider building up a number of language routines with children (see Chapter 6, page 98), e.g. the key person doing the same thing each day with the child or pair of children such as going to feed the fish, laying out the cups or playing a game. In addition, group routines such as singing a 'hello' song each morning or having rhyme times can help children to feel part of the group even if they are not at the stage of joining in.

High levels of facial expression and gesture are needed to aid communication when children are in the early stages of learning a language.

Stage 2: meeting children's needs

- Allow children to stay in proximity to their key person

- Do not force children to repeat phrases or put them under pressure to talk

- Positively acknowledge any communication, e.g. pointing in response to you asking where they want to play

- Talk using simplified language alongside gesture and communication

- Point to key objects and name them

- Use photographs and props and encourage children to take or show you in order to facilitate communication

- Use simple 'language' routines so that children can recognise what is about to happen (see Chapter 6, page 98)

- Create plenty of opportunities for children to join in with small groups or pairs in tasks or play activities.

- Create opportunities for children to be able to demonstrate and get acknowledgement for their competence, e.g. helping themselves to food or putting on their own coats.

Observing the child in the non-verbal stage

The non-verbal period is not a static period and so you should you be checking that the child is making progress in their 'tuning in' to the setting as well as the language. If the child is making progress, you should start to see the following emerge:

- Increasing signs that children feel comfortable within the setting, e.g. smiling, hugging, higher levels of confidence, seeking attention, being cheeky

- Children start to respond to simple instructions or key phrases, e.g. 'snack time'

- Children start to join in with the actions to rhymes and songs or repeated phrases in simple picture books

- Children start to point to objects or pictures in response to simple questions, e.g. 'Where's the ball?'

Decreasing non-verbal communication

You should particularly pay attention to how much non-verbal communication the child is using. If you see that this is starting to decrease, it may be that the child is starting to withdraw which can be a sign of depression or an anxiety response. During this phase, it is important to find out how the child is behaving at home and how parents feel about their child's emotional state.

Formulaic and telegraphic language

In the same way that babies' first words are a cause for celebration, so too are children's first words in English. Few children suddenly speak in whole sentences, but instead are likely to use expressions that they have repeatedly heard such as, 'That's mine!', 'No!' or 'Thank you'. These are formulaic phrases that come in very handy when you first learn a language. Formulaic phrases such as 'What's that?' can also help children to find out more information, whilst 'I want it' can help children to make their needs known.

Telegraphic speech

In the same way that toddlers often use one word to convey several meanings or put two words together to create a mini sentence, so too do children who are new to English. These two word sentences such as 'Apron on' or 'Car down' can convey meaning, but are also the significant steps for the child's progress in understanding the grammatical structure of the language.

Stage 3: meeting children's needs

- Positively acknowledge all communications

- Expand children's telegraphic phrases, e.g. 'Yes, you can have the big trike'

- Give children time to respond to questions or during conversations

- Take time to help children learn words associated with the resources and activities in your setting, e.g. pointing and naming

- Provide language routines which may now include simple questions such as 'What's that?' or 'Where's the....?' to help children show what they know, but also as a way of supplying a word or phrase

- Share simple picture books containing repeated expressions in it, e.g. 'Where's Spot?'

- Use a commentary style so children can hear complete sentences when they are playing or joining in an activity, e.g. 'The car is going down the tube.'

Observing formulaic and telegraphic language

It is worth keeping a record of children's emerging formulaic and telegraphic language. This can be done on a simple sheet. Over a few weeks, you should keep checking that the number of phrases increases. As part of the observation process, you should also make a record of the vocabulary that the child now understands, even if it is not being said. This is worth sharing with parents who may be anxious to check that their child is making progress. You should also use your observations to plan for opportunities to increase vocabulary by, for example, playing picture lotto or using simple picture books.

Productive language

The final stage of learning a new language is the ability to create your own sentences. At first these might be quite short, but they are the next step on the way to fluency. Children's first attempts at productive language are often expansions of their telegraphic or formulaic speech, e.g. 'That's mine' may become 'That trike mine', or 'Look! Spider down there'. This is a very exciting part of the journey and children need to feel that adults and other children are positive about their attempts. For some children who are less outgoing or confident, it may be that their first utterances will be quiet ones, but even if we cannot quite catch what has been said, we need to acknowledge them. It is important not to overtly correct children in this period as to do so may jeopardise their progress.

Over time and with support, children will become increasingly confident and fluent at creating their own sentences and also responding to others. In this phase, children need to hear plenty of commentary-style speech from adults and also be given plenty of time to organise their thoughts so that they can take part in conversations. They will also need to hear their early sentences expanded or correctly recast so that they can learn more.

Over time, it is also important that children are exposed to a range of tenses. In many settings we spend a lot of time talking in the 'here and now', but children will also need to hear the past tense (what has happened) and the future tense (what will happen) so that over time they can start to use them.

We also need to check during this stage that children are correctly ascribing meaning to words and phrases. Many children who are showing productive language may have become quite skilled at looking as if they understand, or good at guessing what a word or phrase means. Checking for comprehension and encouraging children to feel that they can ask 'What does x mean?' is very important.

Books are a useful way of helping bilingual children learn new vocabulary.

Stage 4: meeting children's needs

- Positively acknowledge all interactions and communications

- Do not correct children when they talk or respond

- Allow plenty of time for children to think and formulate their talk

- Recast sentences so that children can hear grammatically correct versions

- Elaborate on simple sentences that children have used

- Share a range of books with children which will help them to acquire new vocabulary and also may help them to hear past tenses

- Repeat activities, books and games for reinforcement of language, but also so children can 'show off' their competence

- Check for children's understanding of phrases and words.

Observing and assessing children's productive language

It is important to keep a record of children's productive language so as to be able to plan new language and vocabulary opportunities. Whilst children's first sentences and attempts at talking are to be celebrated, this is just the start of their journey. There are many ways of recording language acquisition but it can be helpful to create some different categories, e.g. grammatical constructions, sentence complexity, vocabulary areas. The form on the next page might be helpful to use as a starting point in your setting. By making careful observations of children's language use, you can check what progress is being made, but also identify areas that will need modelling or reinforcing.

Reflection points

- How do you maintain children's ability to communicate during the initial stages of acquiring English?

- Does everyone understand the stages of acquiring English, including the role of the adult?

- How are children's emotional needs supported?

- How do you observe and assess children's progress in each of the stages?

- How do you share children's progress in acquiring English with parents?

- How do you plan for children's learning in each of the stages?

Words relating to the routines of the setting, e.g. snack time	Date	Words relating to resources and toys, e.g. sand	Date
Words relating to people and places in setting, e.g. friend, toilet, outside, home	Date	Words relating to people and places home and community, e.g. mummy, flat, street	Date
Social phrases, e.g. please, thank you, bye	Date	Positional vocabulary, e.g. on, in, up, down	Date
Time words, e.g. later, now, in a minute, soon	Date	Action words, e.g. go, come, look	Date
Emotions, e.g. happy, sad, crying, anger	Date	Descriptive words, e.g. nice, ugly, smelly	Date
Questions, e.g. where is?	Date	Sentence use, e.g. 'I want that bike'	Date

Reducing Educational Advantage published by Bloomsbury © Penny Tassoni

Factors affecting children's journey

There are several factors that will affect how quickly children pass through the four stages. As with all aspects of child development, there will be some individual differences between same age children.

Proficiency in home language

Children who have mastered, or nearly mastered, their home language are more likely to pass through the stages of language learning more quickly. This is why it is helpful to gain an understanding of how well the child is talking in their home language on entry to the setting. Proficiency in language means that a four-year-old is likely to start using productive language more quickly than a three-year-old.

Cognition

Learning a new language requires a certain level of cognition. Children have to be able to detect new patterns and rhythms in language and also remember a lot of new information.

Age

Whilst people imagine that very young children will acquire another language more quickly, this is not necessarily the case. It can take a two- or three-year-old longer to pass through the first two stages because: a) they have not yet mastered their home language, and b) their cognitive processing is less developed. In addition, we always have to recognise that for very young children there is a risk that separation from their parents may slow the learning process down because children can become very stressed.

Temperament

In the previous chapter, we looked at temperament in terms of children's communication and language (page 94). For children learning a new language, this is particularly relevant as children who are outgoing and quick to engage with others are likely to have an advantage. This is worth noting early on when a child first comes into a setting, because a child who is less outgoing may need more adult support and input.

Children who are more outgoing are more likely to make faster progress when learning a new language.

Level of support

How much adult support and how well this is delivered can dramatically affect children's progress. A child who attends a setting every day but who has very limited meaningful interaction with adults and other children, is likely to take much longer to acquire English than if the same child is in a sensitive and language-supportive environment.

Exposure

Another significant factor that affects language acquisition is the amount of exposure children are having in the new language. A child who attends for two sessions a week will be slower to acquire English than a child coming every day, assuming that each child is given the same level of support and opportunities to interact.

Motivation

How much a child wants to learn a new language can play a significant role for some children. This can be partly linked to temperament, but also to the circumstances around which the child comes into the setting. Some children may actively refuse to learn a new language. In some cases, this is as a way of protesting against the upheaval of coming to a new country, but for others refusal to engage can be linked to separation anxiety or other emotional issues. It can therefore be worth finding out from parents how their child is feeling about the changes that have taken place in their lives.

Reflection points

- Do you make a note of when code switching (see opposite page) has occurred?

- Do you share this with the parents so that they can provide you with more information for you to be able to support the child's vocabulary?

- Do you share photographs about the routines and events of your setting so that parents can talk about them with children in their home language?

- Do you encourage parents to share photographs of holidays and family events so that you can talk about them with the child in English?

Common issues when children learn more than one language

There are several issues that might arise when you are working with children who are learning two or more languages.

Code switching

This is when children use words or phrases from one language and put them in another. Whilst parents and practitioners can become concerned that the child is becoming confused, this is fairly common and is not a sign that a child has a language delay or disorder. The child is simply being resourceful as the vocabulary needed is missing and so substituting it from another language makes sense. Although this is not a reason for concern, it is worth noting however, because it indicates that the child needs more opportunities to develop the vocabulary for particular interest areas, e.g. a French child talking about a Christmas holiday spent in France might say, 'And I tried a huitre [oyster], but my sister didn't'. If possible, it is always worth noting down what the child was trying to say and seeing if you can find a translation. It is also useful to gain more information from parents and to encourage the sharing of photographs so that you can see or make a guess about what a child might be trying to talk about. Code switching is also likely to occur when the child is speaking their home language in order to explain what has happened in the setting. After all, few homes have 'circle times' or 'gloop'!

Opportunities to maintain home language

The research is clear that maintaining the home language is very beneficial to children's development. It is therefore helpful to look out for books and also DVDs in the child's home language. In situations where no one is able to fluently speak the child's home language, use recorded materials such as talking books. It is also important to encourage parents to keep using the home language as it is not uncommon once the child's exposure to English increases, for the home language to become a receptive one (when the child chooses not to talk using the home language).

Children respond in English rather than the home language at home

When children are increasingly exposed to English, they sometimes stop using their home language with their parents. This can happen quite quickly with children who are simultaneous language learners as the balance of exposure between the languages may have tipped more heavily towards English. This is also more likely when children are spending five or more hours away from their home language. Children may continue to understand the home language, but may only give their responses in English. If this starts to occur, parents should consider increasing their use of the home language, especially if they have been switching between that and English. Some families who have successfully managed this stage also report appearing not to have heard the child's English response, but to be extremely positive when the child rephrases in the home language. For settings, it is worth letting parents know that their child may try to respond only in English at some point, so that they are prepared for this stage. Sadly, if children become used to their parents accepting their responses in English, they quickly lose their ability to be able to talk expressively in their home language.

Supporting parents

One of the ways that we can help all bilingual children is to make sure that we support their parents and provide them with the information that they need to make informed choices. Parents often have a lot of concerns about how best to help their children. I have chosen four of the most common ones to discuss below, alongside some of the issues that they raise.

'We have moved to this country and we want our child to do well.'

For some parents, making the move to a new country and ensuring that their child has a good education is a priority. Many parents believe that to give their child a head start, they will need to speak in English rather than their home language. If parents are very aspirational, it is important that you show them that you have a track record of helping children to develop English and also that you share careful observations and even recordings of the child's progress so that they can 'hear' that their child is doing well. It is worth making the following points;

- Research shows that a strong home language will make it easier for your child to learn English. In addition, having two or more languages can have cognitive advantages

- You can develop your child's cognition further by using your home language. This is because your explanations, discussions and depth of vocabulary are likely to be at a higher level in your home language. This becomes very important in supporting your child with homework later on, especially in subjects such as mathematics and science

- You can support your child's changing emotional and social needs more easily using the 'language of your heart'. This becomes very important when your child is a teenager and you may need to have difficult or sensitive conversations with them. Some families also find that they do not have the same influence over their teenager because of a growing language barrier

- Some teenagers and young adults who have not had the opportunities to learn or maintain their home language become very angry with their parents as they feel that they have been denied opportunities to be fully part of their culture.

'We sometimes use English at home and at other times we use our home language.'

This intermittent use of English is fine, but parents need to know that it may not lead to children mastering the home language for the following reasons:

- Children who have consistency in their home language are more likely to master it and to continue using it even when the exposure to English increases

- Children who learn that their parents will accept either language code, are likely to start responding only in English once they spend more time speaking English as it is likely to become their default language. It can be hard to re-establish talking in the home language once this occurs

- For a few babies and toddlers, inconsistency in the languages that adults use with them can slow down their acquisition of both languages. Although children normally get there in the end and work out which words and grammar belong to which language, it does make things a little harder. For some toddlers who seem to understand well but are slow to talk, it can be worth parents using their home language more consistently.

> *'I speak French, but my partner speaks Polish. We can't speak each other's languages and so we use English as a couple. We want our child to have fluent French and Polish as well as English.'*

This is quite a common situation with parents wanting their children to become fluent in all three languages.

The level of fluency in each language will depend on how much exposure your child has. To ensure that your child has both French and Polish, you should each try to talk as much as possible to your child in your home language. It might be helpful to set up a few routines whereby just one of you interacts with your child, e.g. at bedtime. This means that during these times your child can be fully immersed in either French or Polish with no other distractions. You should also look out for resources such as DVDs and books that again will help your child to be exposed to either French or Polish at any one time.

> *'I am not sure which language to use with my baby. My parents always spoke to us in a mixture of Bengali and English. I use more English than Bengali for my work and in my social life. I want to continue the tradition of Bengali, though.'*

This is becoming a common difficulty as second and third generations of bilinguals find that their home language may not be a fluent language, but they want to maintain the connection between language and culture.

Giving the following advice might be helpful. It is usually best to use the language that you are the most comfortable with and that you can use without any effort or thought. This is important because you need to be totally at ease when you are with your baby so that you can relate to each other. Your relationship with your child is therefore the priority. If you wish to introduce your child to a second language, think about finding a carer or relative who can use this language with your child, although do remember that in order to become fluent, they will need significant exposure to it.

Reflection points

- What knowledge do you have about bilingualism in order to support parents?

- What information do you provide to parents about how best to maintain their home language?

- How do you help parents recognise the progress that their child is making in English?

Summary

In this chapter we have explored the needs of simultaneous as well as sequential bilingual children. We have focused on the importance of understanding how children are being exposed to language and the factors affecting children's acquisition of language. We have also seen that sequential learners appear to go through stages in their language learning and the importance of assessing children's progress particularly during the 'non-verbal' period. In this chapter, I have also looked at information that we might need to provide to parents so that they can make informed choices about their language use at home.

Chapter 8

Creating an environment for early literacy

One of the key ways to close the gap between children is by ensuring that they develop a love of books and have the prerequisite skills needed for reading and writing.

The ability to read and write with ease are skills that many of us take for granted. We may not always fully appreciate their importance in our lives, but the reality is that literacy opens the door to knowledge, self-expression and ultimately self-determination. It is a powerful tool and if we want to make a difference to children's later lives, it is important that we look at ways to support their early literacy development.

Learning to read and write is critical to children's later lives but it takes quite a few years for children to acquire and practise the necessary skills. Contrary to current and previous government policies, the role of early years settings – including the reception class – is not to teach children to read and write, but instead to focus on the background skills that will support this journey. These were traditionally known as 'pre-reading' and 'pre-writing' skills. In this chapter we look primarily at how we might help children to gain pre-reading and pre-writing skills.

Motivation, joy and discovery

One of the starting points when looking at this area is to recognise that motivation, joy and discovery need to be at the forefront of our planning of activities and environments. Learning to read and write is an ongoing task and, as adults, it is easy to forget just how much perseverance and time is needed for children to master them.

T!P

Code-breaking

I often use the following text as a reminder of just how many skills children need to master in early literacy. (If you decide to decode it, don't forget that some capital letters are not the same shape as their lower case equivalents!) A key to three letters has been provided just to get you started.

[encoded symbol text]

CODE:

A = ✌   B = ✊   C = 👍

a = ♋   b = ♌   c = ♍

Children who enjoy handling books, discovering what they can offer and are hungry to read for themselves, are more likely to be motivated to persevere when learning to read. Children who are not highly motivated, despite how good the system and method are, are more likely to fall by the wayside. In the same way, children need to enjoy their first experiences of writing – making marks and having those marks valued for their own sake.

This child's interest in books will help him when he starts to learn to read.

The link between language and literacy

Language and literacy are entwined. It is not possible for children to become literate unless they have mastered language, and so the first priority is always to support children's language. 'Lucky' children begin the process of reading and writing already fluent in the language that they are to be taught in. For most children in the UK, reading and writing is taught in English, although this might not be the case in Wales. Some children pick up on links between sounds and the symbols of letters without fluency, but they often decode without making any sense of what they have decoded. This problem may materialise when it comes to writing, as without being able to speak in full sentences, children will be unable to write them independently. This may all seem obvious, but too often children are being set up for failure by being expected to learn to read and write without having the language to do so. This in turn can lead to children losing their confidence and their motivation. If it were possible to wave a magic wand and change the education system so that reading and writing are introduced when children are ready, outcomes for some children would be very different. Unfortunately, despite numerous campaigns over the years, backed by research evidence that indicates the need to wait, no wand has been waved.

Opportunities to discover books

One of the ways that we can make a real impact on children is to ensure that they have plenty of opportunities to discover and enjoy books. 'Lucky' children are often in book-rich environments, where reading is part of the routine. They get plenty of one-to-one experiences where they pore over a book alongside adults. If a child reads a couple of books in this way most days, it means that they are getting over 700 quality literacy experiences a year. Add this up over three or four years and we soon see that the 'lucky' child will have had several thousand quality reading experiences.

Benefits of sharing books with an adult one-to-one

When we look at the benefits that children gain from reading books one-to-one with an adult, we really start to see just what an advantage the 'lucky' child has. Not only will these children know how books work with print running from left to right, but they are likely to want to access this land of print for themselves. They are also likely to already have favourite books, and as a result many children will have started to recognise some words that are important for them, e.g. 'Gruffalo' or 'hungry' as in *The Very Hungry Caterpillar*. Children also start to see themselves as readers and participants in the telling of the story. The one-to-one shared book experience means that children can make connections between what is on the page and their own experiences or knowledge. They may point to a picture of a child wearing a blue jumper and say, 'My brother has a blue jumper just like that'. They may also ask questions about why things have happened or what the characters are doing. The learning that comes from sharing a book with an adult is more than just literacy itself. The attention that children need from adults is usually undiluted or uninterrupted and thus intense, meaning that the potential associated learning is immense.

Group stories are not substitutes

Whilst group stories can supplement individual book sharing times, they are not a substitute for the experience that children gain when looking carefully at a book alone (or with one other child at a push.) Group stories by their very nature cannot be so personally tailored to the individual child. The style of reading the adult adopts changes and the book is usually read in a linear fashion and with minimum discussion. This is inevitable, since long conversations or questions that may be of interest to one child may result in others losing their concentration. Group stories do not enable children to pore over the print and delve into illustrations, as even big books held by an adult are likely to be too far away. This means that whilst they do have some impact, relying on group stories alone to help children discover the world of books is not likely to be sufficient for children whose only book experiences are from within our setting.

Group stories are useful, but are not a substitute for a one-on-one story.

Making shared books happen

Assuming that we all believe that one-to one-personalised opportunities to share a book with an adult make a difference, I would argue that this needs to be a major focus for adult-led activity. The ideal would be for every child to have one shared book a day. I know that this can be a challenge in group settings.

You should start by focusing on certain children who you suspect may not have opportunities for books at home or written in the language of your setting. In settings with large numbers of children who need this opportunity, you may have to compromise and do this with pairs of children. Sometimes, to achieve this, you may need to reconsider routines and think carefully about how to deploy adults. In schools where adult-child ratios are not favourable, it may mean petitioning for additional adults on the basis that if this work is done, it will improve the dreaded data. Schools may also like to consider using older children to share stories with younger ones. This has been quite effective in many schools as it helps some older children gain confidence whilst acting as positive role models for younger ones.

Tracking one-to-one shared stories

'Lucky' children have access to a wide range of books. Not only do they have regular favourites, but they are also exposed to books that widen their knowledge.

You might consider creating a tracking system for the books that you share on a one-to-one or paired basis, as this is such precious learning time it should be used to full effect. By creating some sort of a tracking system, you can ensure that children are given opportunities to explore the full range of benefits that books provide. You may also begin to see that children develop favourite types of books. Please note that whilst I do advocate a tracking system this is not at the expense of children missing out on choosing favourites ones again and again.

You might, therefore, want to track the type and range of books with a view to ensuring that over a period of a few months, children have enjoyed a wide range of books that are appropriate for their level of development, including fiction and non-fiction.

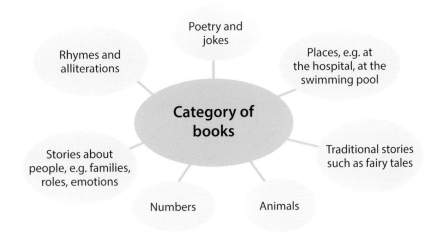

Sharing a book works best when both the adult and the child are enjoying it.

Shared enjoyment

Whether or not you put a tracking system in place, it is essential to make sure that the books you choose appeal to adults and children alike. This is because when adults enjoy a book, they read it with more enthusiasm and feeling and, crucially, they take their time. They don't skip pages or paraphrase large chunks and whizz through it. This may seem obvious, but it is surprising how many settings have books in them that the adults do not enjoy reading to the children. Sometimes these books have been 'handed down' to the setting when a family has had a clear out or picked up because the cover has a superhero or television character on it. Sadly, the usual reason why these books don't work for adults is because they are not beautifully written and/or illustrated. Whilst I recognise the importance of picking up on children's interests, when it comes to books, adults need to be judicious on children's behalf. Interestingly, children's favourite books, of which they never tire, are often closely connected to the adults who read them!

Reflection points

- How many stories do you read one-to-one or in pairs to all your children each week?

- How are books selected for shared reading?

- Do you provide information to parents about which books their children have enjoyed?

- How often do you visit the library with children?

- Are the books in your provision of high quality and developmentally appropriate?

- How do you track children's progress and interest in sharing books?

- Do you provide 'successful' books for parents to share at home?

Specific skills associated with reading

As well as creating opportunities for children to explore the wonderful world of books, children also need specific pre-reading skills that will help them when they start to read.

Experience of rhymes

Spoken language is key to learning to read and write, but children of all ages also benefit from extensive exposure to rhymes. Hearing rhymes, patterns and individual sounds in words seems to help with children's later ability to learn letter-sound associations. Regardless of whichever teaching method for reading comes in and out of fashion, the need to make letter-sound associations will always be a reading strategy. Rhymes also have other benefits – they help children's speech production, and for children who do not have English, they can help them hear the sounds of the language.

Whilst most early years settings do recite some rhymes with their children, it is worth considering putting a programme of rhymes together. Otherwise, the danger is that children may keep repeating the same few rhymes, rather than learning new ones. Although there is no 'magic' number of rhymes that children have to acquire, it would seem that quantity does help and every rhyme will give children a slightly different experience.

When I work with settings, I suggest that they set a realistic target of rhymes to introduce to children each year. If children are exposed to 20 new rhymes a year, this equates to around two per month. As many children will be with us for two years, this then means that they can move into a reception class with 40 or so rhymes. As well as planning for children's rhymes, it may also be worth assessing children's progress in learning them. You may start to see which children pick up rhymes very quickly and which children need more reinforcement.

Choosing rhymes

As with sharing books, the best rhymes to share with children are ones that the adults enjoy. This means that if you want to construct a rhyming

programme, it is a good idea for everyone to be involved in the selection process. Where children are in the same room for two years, e.g. an age 2-4 room, it is worth devising a two-year rolling programme rather than divide children into separate groups, because in the end, it does not matter in which order children learn different rhymes.

Ideally, it would be a good idea to include rhymes that involve counting as well as those that have specific alliterations. It is also worth looking at traditional rhymes, as they tend to have strong rhythms and sounds – which of course is why they have survived for so long! These rhymes do need to be carefully selected though, as some are offensive by today's standards.

For children due to start on a phonic programme, it is also worth programming in rhymes in their final weeks that link to the first sounds that they will be taught. In many programmes, the initial sounds for teaching are S-A-T-P-I-N so 'She Sells Seashells on the Seashore' might work well, as might 'Five little Peas in a Peapod Pressed'!

Sharing rhymes

There was a period of time when rhymes fell seriously out of fashion. This means that there are a couple of generations of adults who do not know many nursery rhymes. It is therefore worth finding ways of sharing rhymes with adults, including staff and parents. Some settings that take a planned approach to teaching children rhymes, send home the words of rhymes or recordings of the rhymes being recited. Recordings are often more effective as it is always easier to learn a rhyme by hearing it rather than just by seeing it written down. For parents who do not have English as their first language, hearing the rhyme will be particularly helpful. As well as sharing English rhymes, we may also want to encourage parents who speak other languages to record rhymes or songs in their home language. This is not only a way of valuing other languages, but it adds to children's overall phonemic awareness.

Reflection points

- How many rhymes will your children know when they leave your setting?

- Do you track children's progress in rhymes?

- Do you include some rhymes from children's home languages?

- How do you share rhymes with parents?

- Do you choose rhymes that will support the reading programme of the local school/s?

Rhymes help children's phonemic awareness.

Sound games

A few years ago, the then National Strategy team produced a 'Letters and Sounds' pack that had plenty of activities and games to help children develop phonemic awareness. Whilst this material has been archived, it is still accessible online and it is a great starting point for ideas of sound games. (Put the key words National Strategy Letters and Sounds 2007 in a search engine.)

T!P

Sound games

I Spy games	• Use letter sounds and when children are ready the letter names.
Kim's game (see Chapter 9, page 167)	• Use objects that have the same initial sound.
Odd one out	• Have three objects or pictures that rhyme and one that does not.
Clapping games	• Can children join in with a clapping pattern? • Can they clap out the beats in their name?
Initial sound game game	• Each child is given a letter sound and they must stand when they hear that sound.
Sorting into groups	• Children sort objects into groups according to their initial sound.
Putting sounds together to make words	• A group of objects (that are phonetically spelt) are put out on a tray, e.g. hat, tin, rabbit. The adult sounds out the name of the object, e.g. h-a-t. The children have to point to the correct object.

Matching games

Children also benefit from games where they have to match pairs or find shared characteristics, e.g. spot the difference cards, pairs and picture lotto. In Chapter 9 (page 150) we look at these in more detail as they also support children's cognitive development. In terms of learning to read, children need to be able to recognise and remember letter shapes and also spot similarities between words. It is therefore important to plan and play games that build on these skills. As children make progress, you could also consider matching games that have words or letter shapes on them, e.g. picture lotto that has been adapted so that a few words are included.

Telling a story

Being able to retell a familiar story or to use pictures to create a story is a traditional pre-reading skill. It supports children's language development, but also helps them to recognise sequences in the language. Traditionally, first books for children did not contain any words. Instead, children would sit with an adult and look at the pictures and create a possible story together. Telling a story in this way is, in my view, an essential pre-reading activity and opportunities for this should be planned into your programme. This, along with assessment, impacts upon children's growing confidence and skill.

Reflection points

- How often do children tell or retell a story?

- Do you have resources such as story sacks to encourage story telling?

- How do you track and assess children's progress in story telling?

Storytelling helps children learn about sequencing.

Print awareness

'Lucky' children have adults who point out signage in the local environment as well as on products at home. Early print awareness can support both writing and early reading. There are many ways of supporting this in settings, but one of the most obvious is to use captions and labels. If you decide to do this, it is important to draw children's attention to these labels. Ideally, you should put up labels that will appeal to children as they are more likely to remember and focus on the letter shapes. Whilst few children are genuinely interested in a sign that says 'door', or 'table', they may be more alert to a nonsense sign that says 'dandy door' or 'ticklish table'. Signs can also be made using children's suggestions, and this is one way of helping them to become interested in the sounds in words.

As well as using signs and captions, print awareness can come through the resources that we have available, but again, we do need to make sure that we draw children's attention to them. Look out for alphabets in a variety of formats, including jigsaws. Alphabets can help children develop an interest in letter shapes, particularly if they learn an alphabet song alongside them.

Reflection points

- Where are the opportunities for children to see words as print in your setting?

- How do you help children to notice them?

- Do you regularly change labels, captions and resources to maintain interest?

- Do you have resources that help children to see and engage with the alphabet?

Learning to write

Children are often expected to write before they have fully mastered the basics of reading. This has only recently become the case and I have found that it does not work for many children. This approach places children in situations where they know they cannot be successful. Traditional pre-writing skills have always focused on developing children's interest in mark making and on motor skills, rather than on the actual process of writing.

Motivating children

One of the most important pre-writing tasks that we need to focus on is encouraging children's interest in writing. Without motivation and feelings of success, children are less likely to practise the skills and to fully engage in the learning process. One of the key mistakes that many adults make with young children is to focus too much on their early products and efforts. Advice, correction and even praise can make children wary of writing. They may learn that writing is something that is judged and that adults like to be correct. This can lead to children who are doing well on their writing journey reducing the time they spend engaged in writing or only repeating letters and words that they feel confident are correct. Ironically, it is through experimentation that children are more likely to learn the link between letters and sounds and so an over-zealous approach can actually backfire. Interested and sensitive adults who share children's enthusiasm and are not 'judging products' during the mark making and writing process are more likely to facilitate early writing.

Satisfying mark making opportunities

For our youngest children, early writing is all about tactile experiences referred to as mark making. Children want to make their mark and this can be seen from aged six months when babies start to enjoy smearing food onto highchair trays or turning beakers of drink upside down and putting their fingers into the liquid. Early mark making experiences are important for a variety of reasons, including the development of hand-eye co-ordination and the development of muscles in the arms and hands. It is important that children experience a range of tactile mark making experiences that will feel satisfying and will therefore motivate them to write. Although at first it is helpful if children use their hands only, as children become more co-ordinated, mark making experiences will also need to include tools such as sticks, brushes and rollers.

Mark making needs to feel satisfying for children.

Mark making ideas

Sensory materials/resources	Tools
Sand – dry, damp	Brushes, e.g. toothbrushes, nail brushes shaving brushes, mushroom brushes, hair brushes
Couscous, rice or lentils	Combs
Hair gel	Cotton buds (supervise carefully)
Shaving foam	Rollers of different sizes
Gloop	Lollipop sticks
Paint in trays or spread out on a table	Sponges
Water in a bucket	Cars
Whiteboards	Large chalks and markers
Magic slate boards	Plastic pencils
Magna Doodle/ Aquadoodle™	Brushes, pens

Steps in mark making

The first stages of mark making are very exploratory. If children have had their attention drawn little by little to print, we should see the emergence of letter shapes. It is important that we track children's progress in mark making and that we note which children are starting to show an interest in forming letters. It is also important that even when children are starting to use letter shapes that they are encouraged to continue using the tactile materials rather than using pencils and markers exclusively. This can prevent children from developing a poor hand grasp and it can also keep their movements fluid, as most tactile mark making experiences are done on a large scale. (See 'Writing movements' page 148)

Reflection points

- How are children's steps in mark making tracked?

- How are staff members and parents helped to understand the stages of mark making?

- What information is given to parents about how they can support mark making at home?

Mark making examples

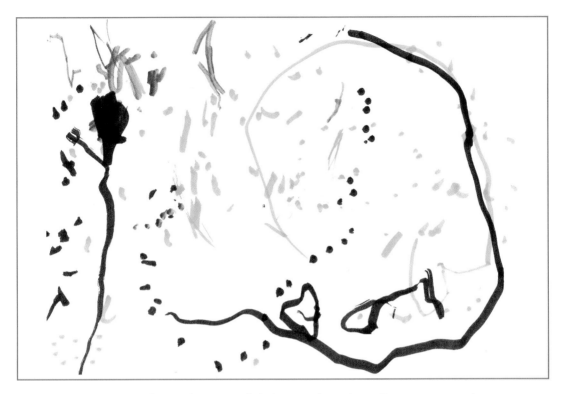

Most children begin with making exploratory marks before using letter shapes. To support progression, children need plenty of opportunities to see print in a meaningful way.

Role modelling 'manual' writing

As well as enjoying mark making as a tactile experience, older children are motivated to write when watching adults do so. Shopping lists, letters and notes on a calendar used to be commonplace experiences for children to observe. In the age of screen technology and mobile phones, few children see the key adults in their lives engage in pen and paper writing on a regular basis. This in turn has meant that many groups of children do not have the same motivation to write in this way. In particular, some boys may reach the conclusion that pen and paper writing is for girls if they have only seen women write in this way, which may be the case in all female early years settings.

Children are often motivated to write because they want to copy what adults do.

T!P

Where to encourage writing

- Pirates' dens

- Fairy castles

- 'Boardroom meetings' with diaries, calculators and envelopes

- 'Inventors laboratories' with secret formulas

- Kitchens where new recipes are recorded

- Takeaway restaurants where telephone orders are written down

- Explorer bags which contain maps, pens and notebooks

- Painters and decorators where shades of paint have to be named and written down

- Cake-making business where dough cakes are made, named and orders taken

- Santa's grotto, where letters are written and received before presents are wrapped.

As manual writing is the first way in which children learn to write, it is important therefore that we spend a lot of time in settings modelling writing so that children become motivated to join in. We may also need to be creative in helping children who are not so motivated to feel that writing can be fun. A good example of this is the way that many settings have success with some boys when they 'masculinise' writing opportunities for boys by, for example, putting out hard hats, tool boxes and clipboards. The win-win scenario often occurs when adults model writing in the creative environments that they have created to engage children.

Reflection points

- How often do you spend time writing alongside children?

- Do you work with parents to help them understand the importance of modelling writing?

- Do you look for ways of helping boys to see that writing is for them?

Having a personal scribe

Children need opportunities to see their spoken words and sentences written down. The benefits of scribing for children are significant. Firstly, it helps children learn the link between the spoken word and print. It is also an empowering process for the child who can see that their words are important. Through the process of sensitive scribing, children can draw attention to the sounds in words and also the way that certain letter shapes are constructed. They also see how print in English is put down from left to right, and from top to bottom. One of the key benefits of scribing activities is that children are more likely to revisit what has been written and so develop a heightened awareness of print. There are many ways in which scribing opportunities can be planned or suggested in response to a child's activity, e.g.

- Making a book with a child or small group of children
- Scribing captions to go with children's drawings, paintings and 3D models
- Scribing messages that a child can give to a parent, member of staff or another child
- Scribing captions for photographs.

Role of the adult when scribing

When scribing for children it is essential that adults are sensitive during the process. Many children will need time to process and consider what they want to say. They may also change their mind or not sequence things accurately. Adults have to be careful not to put words into children's mouths or take over the process. As with all skills, the more opportunities children have to dictate, the easier they will find using the words. To help children learn about sounds from scribing activities, adults can change the colour of pen for each word that they write, thus helping children to see letters in blocks, and words as whole units of sound or, if adults are focusing on a particular letter sound, they may write that single sound in a different colour.

Reflection points

- How often do you create opportunities for adults to scribe for children?

- Do adults take time to use scribing opportunities to help children learn more about print and also letters and sounds?

Handwriting

It is important to remember that handwriting is a tool for writing. It is not writing in itself. After all, people can write using a keyboard, touching a screen or even using voice-activated technology. Having said that, writing by hand is the entry point for most children when learning to write. As such, it is important that we help to prepare children for this. Interestingly, handwriting begins with large gross motor movements and then moves on to fine motor movements, and this is why mark making opportunities should be expansive to start with. There is also a range of movements that children should be taught in order that they can eventually form letter shapes correctly.

Hand preference

Most children should be showing consistent hand preference at aged two and a half. It is often one of those overlooked areas of development, but it is important in early writing. Some children develop a strong hand preference very easily, but other children may benefit from activities that will strengthen hand preference. It is worth noting, that adults cannot choose a hand preference for a child as this is biologically predetermined. Indeed, there will always be some children with mixed-handedness. Having said this, some activities can reinforce a weak pre-existing preference. These activities work by encouraging each hand to take on a different function: stabilising or active. A good example of an active/stabilising movement would be threading beads. When threading a bead, one hand has to hold the bead (stabiliser) whilst the other hand (active) does the threading. The idea is that by increasing the number and frequency of these activities, a weak hand preference can be strengthened. Many of the activities that work in this way were part of traditional household life when children were given tasks and responsibilities. The list above shows examples of everyday activities that can help to strengthen hand preference.

T!P

Everyday activities to determine hand preference

- Using a dustpan and brush
- Peeling a banana or a satsuma
- Threading beads or simple sewing activities
- Using scissors
- Construction play
- Pouring a drink whilst holding the cup.
- Washing, drying up, cleaning small equipment such as Duplo™ bricks with a toothbrush
- Cooking activities, e.g. cutting, spreading, grating mixing
- Laying a table, pegging up laundry
- Junk modelling, collage activities.

Activities involving a hand that is stable and a hand that is active can strengthen hand preference.

Pencil grasp

One of the consequences of introducing writing too early is that children are often encouraged to write with pencils before they have established a dynamic tripod grasp. This is the grasp that is considered to be most effective when joining letters and writing at speed.

As this grasp takes a while to develop, it is important that children under four spend a lot of time using materials other than pencils or 'stick-like' tools. This means that they do not develop a habit of using a less effective pencil grasp. In order for children to progress to the dynamic tripod grasp, they need a lot of early hand activity that will strengthen the muscles associated with this grasp especially the pincer grasp movement. There are many resources and tools that you can use to help children gain this skill, although it is worth starting with activities that involve only the hand rather than a tool. The good news is that when children are practising these movements, they are also developing hand–eye co-ordination and strengthening the muscles in their hands.

Developing the pincer grasp movement

Examples of activities	Examples of resources
Placing chickpeas and sequins in a bowl	Clothes pegs
Picking up coins and dropping them into a piggy bank	Pipettes
Folding paper to make a fan	Tweezers
Pulling drinking straws out from dough	Peg boards
Putting spots (plastics counters) onto a template of a ladybird	Beads and laces

Early writing movements

Early writing movements help build children's control and co-ordination, but they also help to develop motivation and confidence. Working on some of the early writing movements is particularly important as many schools start off with either full cursive or partial cursive handwriting in the reception class. The flicks and joins in cursive handwriting require children to have developed flexible movements and rhythms in their writing. Children who have done a lot of tracing activities are more likely to find these movements harder to make as tracing activities, including 'dotted letters', restrain children's movements and so encourage them to become less flexible in their movements.

There are four distinct movements that can help children prepare for correct letter formation (see opposite). Ideally, these four movements should be in place before children are encouraged to write words using lower case letters. If children are encouraged to copy or write words without having acquired these movements, they are more likely to develop some poor letter formation habits. These can take a long while to reverse, especially when the letters occur in their names. If there is a lot of pressure from parents and others for children to start writing their names, it is probably better if they do so using capitals. The reality is that capitals are easier for children to form and they are less likely to produce them inaccurately.

Helping children to acquire the essential writing movements

Children learn better when they are having fun. This means that the five writing movements should be taught with interesting materials and ideally in a playful manner that encourages children to use gross motor movements. The starting point is to model the movements. A painting wall or a large sheet of paper on a wall can work well because then the adult can model first and the child can have a go afterwards, underneath or next to the adult's. Games such as 'follow my leader' work well for this. In addition, the movements can be done on trays using brushes, e.g. coloured dry rice and a brush. Movements can also be practised using scarves in time to music. It is only when children have developed sufficient control that these movements should be encouraged on a smaller scale.

The four distinct movements for writing

Vertical strokes
Some letter shapes begin with a vertical stroke that goes from the top down to the bottom. Good examples of letter shapes that do this are the 'b', 'd', 'h' and 'i'.

Anti-clockwise rotational marks
Some letter shapes begin with an anti-clockwise movement that begins at the top. Letters include 'c' and 'd' but also the start of the 'f' and 's'. This is an important movement to assess, as many children will form circular shapes from the bottom. Left-handed children are also more likely to travel clockwise.

Bouncing movements
Bouncing movements which form arches are also important for children to master. Over arches include the 'n' and also the 'm'. Under arching movements are needed for letters such as the 'u' and 'y', but also to form the joins between letters for joined handwriting.

'Doubling back'
Once children have mastered the bouncing movements, it is helpful if they learn to double back on themselves as this little movement is used in forming a variety of letters, e.g. a lower case 'm' as well as when joining letters e.g. th.

Putting the movements together to form letters

Once children have acquired the different movements, it is then possible to show them how to produce the individual letters . This is because most letter shapes are a composition of these movements, e.g. the 'h' is produced by the vertical movement, a doubling back and then a bouncing movement. As most children are interested in their names, it makes sense to start with one or two of the letters in their names.

Reflection points

- Are opportunities to learn the handwriting movements provided in your writing programme?

- How often do children practise these movements?

- How is progress in the movements assessed?

- Are these movements shared with parents?

Summary

In this chapter we have looked at early literacy and its links to fluent language. We have explored the importance of children having 1:1 and 1:2 shared book reading with adults in order that they develop a love of books, but also as a way to extend vocabulary and knowledge of the world.

We have also seen that learning to read and write is related to children developing early skills including phonemic awareness, rhyming knowledge, a knowledge of print as well as fine motor movements. As a result of this chapter, you may like to consider the extent to which you strategically plan for these early skills and, in particular whether you should focus on children having access to 1:1 or 1:2 shared stories.

Chapter 9

Cognition, problem-solving and mathematics

In order to close the gap between groups of children, we have to turn our attention to cognitive function.

'Lucky' children have adults who explain, show and draw attention to interesting details. They also encourage children to problem-solve, reason and articulate their thoughts. 'Lucky' children also learn about counting, number and shape alongside adults and through the type of games that adults play with them. This, coupled with strong levels of language, gives these children a significant head start. If we want to support children at risk of disadvantage, it is therefore important to think about how we can give children opportunities to develop a range of skills associated with cognition within the subject area of mathematics.

In this chapter, we look at how we can provide opportunities to support children's cognitive development and help them develop problem-solving and mathematical thinking skills.

Links to language

Whilst cognition is closely linked to brain development and growth, there is also a connection between language and cognition. Being able to use language seems to open doors when it comes to thinking. It allows children to process and store information, but also to make conscious connections between the information that has been stored. A child may see a ball and say, 'That's like my ball, but it's not because mine doesn't have spots on it.' Strong language levels are also linked to children's ability to plan and evaluate. This often reveals itself when children are playing. They may decide beforehand what the 'story' is when in the home corner or whilst building a tower using bricks they may think about why the roof won't stay on. The link to language is one reason why opportunities for language development need to be focused on when planning in the early years.

Vocabulary counts

One of the aspects of language that can help children's cognition and their ability to process information is their vocabulary. Individual words are like shades of colours. The more shades of colour that you can see, the more colourful and interesting the world becomes. The child who knows the words 'parka', 'duffle coat' and 'denim jacket' will be seeing and thinking about coats differently from children who just have a single word; 'coat'. This is because individual words tend to draw our attention to the features of an object or subject of conversation. Interestingly, this in turn means that children who have a wide vocabulary are more accurate in how they are able to process and store information. This allows them to take in more from any new experience or situation. It also allows them to spot the differences and shared characteristics between their new experience and past ones.

Identifying children who may need support with vocabulary

Although we should of course be helping all children to build their vocabulary, it is important that we do identify and focus on those children who may, for a variety of reasons, need to acquire more vocabulary. Whilst we have already looked at the need for bilingual children to develop vocabulary across languages in Chapter 8, we should also be aware that children who are in danger of being overlooked can sometimes be those who are actually quite chatty. This is because we tend to assume that talkative children are gaining vocabulary automatically. It is therefore worth listening carefully to the responses of children when they need to explain or analyse, to check whether they have the vocabulary bank that they need. Questions such as, 'I wonder why you don't like eating this?' or 'Why do you think you like playing with sand so much?' are often quite revealing because they require children to use language to explain their thinking.

Adults need to help children develop vocabulary by accurately using specific words that describe features and details of objects.

Developing language for thinking

In a previous version of the EYFS, the English early years curriculum, 'language for thinking' was a specific aspect. Whilst linguists and others would no doubt question whether 'language for thinking' can be separated in this way, I have always found this term to be helpful and preferable to the term 'sustained shared thinking' that is currently used. 'Language for thinking' highlights the difference between using language to communicate as opposed to using language in order to explain, analyse, predict and reflect. Language for thinking can be developed in a variety of ways, so it is worth reflecting on these:

Modelling vocabulary – drawing children's attention to detail

We have seen in the chapter on communication and language (Chapter 6, page 86) that modelling language is a key way in which adults can support children's overall acquisition of language. When it comes to helping children acquire detailed and precise vocabulary, modelling is once more one of the tools needed. Using modelling, we can draw children's attention to specific words and in doing so draw their attention to detail. This in turn helps them to see the world differently and process information more accurately. This can happen casually as you comment on a child's stripy cardigan or the pith on the piece of orange that they are eating.

Modelling logic and reason – 'a window into the mind'

One of the ways that adults can help children's cognition and language is to talk aloud so that they are literally hearing an adult's thinking process. In effect, children get a chance to see into the workings of an adult's mind. If you were picking up a coat from the floor, you might say aloud, 'I'll pick this up otherwise it might get dirty', or if you were setting up a mark making table, you might say, 'I think I'll put more paper out as there are more children in today.' Casually sharing your thoughts with children seems to help them learn to see connections between actions and can also influence how they think over time.

Questioning and commenting

Sensitive questioning and comments can help children to hear and practise the skills of language for thinking. It is important that questions are timed carefully and are said in ways that do not sound like an interrogation. Comments such as, 'I wonder why you enjoy that book' often work better with some children than the more direct, 'Why do you like that book?'. This indirect way of asking a question also allows you to suggest some answers if it becomes clear that the child might not have the language to respond, e.g. 'Perhaps it is the pictures you like, or perhaps you like the way that it rhymes?'

By commenting or using questions, adults can extend children's thinking and learning.

Reflection points

- How do you assess children's vocabulary?

- Do you plan specific opportunities to help children hear new words and phrases in context?

- Do you use precise language routinely in context?

Contexts

In many ways, developing children's language for thinking relies more on the adult's style of interaction than on any given context. This means that developing children's language and opportunities for thought can happen anywhere and at any time.

Spontaneously

Ideally, a lot of language for thinking should be taking place spontaneously, as this is partly about the style in which we work with children. The spontaneous approach works well when it centres around children's interests. This is because a child who is already interested in an activity or has seen something that attracted their attention, is more likely to be receptive to learning or thinking further about it. A child may be rolling cars down some guttering and want to show the adult how fast they travel down. The adult can then develop language for thinking by saying, 'How interesting. I wonder whether it makes a difference to the speed if the car has wide tyres' and then point to the tyres. This may then take the child and the adult's thinking in a new direction. In a similar way, an adult might support a baby who has reached the pointing phase of communication development by correctly naming the object that the baby is pointing to before elaborating a little further.

Everyday routines

Many routine activities that children are familiar with, such as tidying up or washing their hands, can become great language for thinking opportunities. It is particularly useful to identify those activities that have become mundane and automatic for children and look for ways of using them to develop children's learning. This can be anything from encouraging children to look at the way water travels down plug holes to seeing whether children can drop plastic bricks into their storage box without making any sound when tidying up.

Washing hands is an everyday routine but it is possible to make it a useful learning opportunity.

Opportunities to develop language for thinking in everyday routines

Tidying toys	Encourage children to think about the reasons for tidying and sorting objects according to colour, size and shape.
	• What would happen if we left everything out?
	• Why are boxes for storage square or rectangular in shape?
	• Is there a difference in the amount of space taken if items are stacked/folded as opposed to put in randomly?
Washing up	Encourage children to explore water and its use for cleaning.
	• Why does water travel downwards?
	• What happens when water and something greasy come in contact with each other?
	• Does hot water make any difference to washing up liquid's efficacy?
Dustpan and brush	Encourage children to look at how objects move when touched.
	• Why are larger objects easier to sweep up than smaller ones?
	• Does it make any difference if smaller strokes are used?
	• Are there any objects that roll away when brushed?

Reflection points

● How do you use everyday routines in order to support children's thinking?

● Do you observe and assess children's language for thinking?

Adult-led activities to support cognition

As well as using spontaneous opportunities and everyday routines to develop children's language for thinking, it is also important to plan activities and opportunities that will foster logic, and give children early mathematical experiences.

It is also important to recognise that good adult-led activities should be compatible with child-initiated provision as the experiences, language and associated thinking gained can give children more ways of developing their play, as well as more avenues for developing interests with the support of adults. The EPPE project (see Introduction, <XREF>) reported that an equal amount of adult-led and child-initiated activities were a feature of high-quality provision and that those settings also placed an emphasis on early mathematics, early science and early literacy.

Specific activities and opportunities

There are some activities and opportunities which will require adult input that are worth focusing on. Although they may occur spontaneously, I still see them as 'adult-led', as without the adult input, children may not develop skills. It is worth identifying children who may benefit from these activities and opportunities.

Opportunities to practise sequencing

One of the adult-led activities that children need to develop is sequencing. Putting events, stories, photographs or pictures into order can promote memory skills, and also logic. Some children have plenty of practice with this as their parents or other key people in their lives take time to listen and talk together about what they have done. Planning opportunities for children to do this is important. It can take place in a variety of ways including encouraging children to look at a series of photographs taken during an activity or outing that they enjoyed or together retelling a story that has been read. It is also possible to make cards that show several steps of a story or a routine activity, such as getting dressed, and seeing if the children can work out the order.

Supporting sequencing by listening

Children need adults to listen to their stories and explanations of what they have been doing. This means that one of the most important advice for adults is to give children time and not to rush in to take over from them. Some children need to talk a lot before they will be ready to come to a conclusion about the order of events. Some children will also need us to model the language used to help with sequencing, e.g. first, next and finally. To help children sequence, there may also be times when we need to ask questions to help children work out the order, or to recap so that they can hear the order.

Looking at photographs and putting them in order can help children learn to sequence events.

Opportunities for children to practise sequencing could include:

- Talking about an activity or event that has just taken place.

- Using photographs of an activity or event and putting them in order.

- Encouraging children to talk about the process needed to do routine activities, such as getting their coat, preparing for a meal or finding their shoes.

Reflection points

- How do you support children's sequencing skills?

- Do you provide specific opportunities and activities that will require sequencing?

- Do you model the language of sequencing, e.g. 'first', 'second', 'then'?

- How do you help parents to recognise opportunities for sequencing conversations with their children, e.g. reviewing their trip to the corner shop or what happened the day that they moved home?

Construction play

The value of construction play is well-documented. It gives children first-hand experience of handling shapes, problem-solving and also learning about structures. Many types of construction play can allow children to be creative and to learn to plan projects. Children can benefit emotionally from this type of play as they gain satisfaction from overcoming problems. Although most early years settings have a range of construction toys, not all children can access them or are able to benefit from having an adult engage with them. 'Lucky' children not only have access to these toys, but also have opportunities to enjoy construction alongside an adult who can develop their play and thinking. As part of construction experiences, we also need to plan for opportunities to build large structures such as dens and use construction to solve problems, such as building a bridge to prevent an area of grass from becoming muddy.

Supporting construction play

It is important to begin by identifying those children who rarely access construction type play. There are many reasons why this may happen, although it is worth being aware that some girls from age three onwards do not always see this type of play as being for them. Other children

Construction play has many cognitive benefits for young children.

may start on a project but may not have the experience or skills to complete what they set out to achieve. As construction play is hugely beneficial, it is important that we help children to enjoy this type of play. This may require us to work in a variety of ways. Firstly, for some children who are competent in this type of play, our role may be that of an interested co-worker who is ready to take orders. In this role, we may ask for clarification as to why things are being done and to note children's explanations. For children who come to an area with a project in mind, but without the skills or sequencing knowledge to achieve it, our role may be that of a facilitator. We may gently suggest, explain or show, in order to help the child or children finish what they have started. Then there are children who are construction novices. They may have tried in the past, but given up because they have not developed the manipulative skills, knowledge or motivation to continue. Our role here is likely to be a little more directive, and so effectively the children become active apprentices in an enjoyable activity, learning as they go.

There are many different types of construction activities and resources that benefit children. Ideally, children will learn most from experiencing a range of these activities alongside an adult.

Construction activities and resources

Duplo™ and Lego™	• Interlocking bricks allow for more stable and thus potentially more complex structures to be built.
Jigsaws	• Help children to learn to sequence a task, differentiate between shapes and support spatial awareness.
Junk modelling	• Supports problem-solving, trial and error learning and exploration of the difference between materials and textures. • Also supports children's developing concepts of size, shape and measurement.
Making large structures, e.g. dens	• Helps children to learn how materials and resources combine. • Encourages problem-solving and gives children first-hand experience of shape, size and measuring.
Block play	• Allows children to create structures using natural materials. • Fosters creativity and helps children to actively choose and explore size and shapes.

Reflection points

● Do you have a wide range of construction materials including jigsaws that will increasingly challenge children?

● How do you ensure that all children use construction materials?

● How do you help children to make increasingly complex structures or solve problems?

● Do you encourage children to talk about their goals as well as any potential barriers to meeting them?

● How do you assess children's approach to problem-solving and how they progress within it?

Playing mathematical games

'Lucky' children often have access to games that help them develop thinking skills including logic and some early mathematical skills. They may play board games or card games such as 'snap' with their families. Playing mathematical games benefits children in other ways too, as they learn to co-operate with others and practise self-regulation skills, which may include learning to lose a game. Most games also encourage hand-eye skills and fine manipulative movements. One of great things about playing mathematical games with children is that if we choose the right level of game for their development, it is likely to be a highly pleasurable activity for them. They may also choose to play it, and so many games thus become child-initiated.

Using mathematical games to develop logic and thinking

It is important that children benefit from hearing adults think. This means that adults need to take part in mathematical games and narrate their thoughts, e.g. counting aloud or explaining their logic. Hearing adults in this way seems to affect the way that children play and the speed at which they acquire effective strategies.

Traditional games are a great way of helping children develop logic as well as other mathematical skills.

Games to develop logic and thinking

Snap	• Good for matching skills. • Good for comparing the number of cards between players.
Dominos	• Helps children to count and match numbers.
Picture lotto	• Good for matching skills. • Good for one-to-one correspondence.
Kerplunk or similar games	• Provides opportunities for children to develop strategy and learning about cause and effect. • Provides counting opportunities during and after the game.
Ludo type games	• Helps children to recognise numbers on a dice. • Gives children opportunities to count as they move counters. • Good for developing strategies.
Beetle drive/build a beetle game	• Helps children to recognise numbers.
Tumbling blocks, e.g. Jericho, Jenga	• Develops positional language, strategy and trial by learning.
Happy families	• Helps children to build sets, count, use memory and also strategy.

Reflection points

- How many mathematical games are regularly played with children in your setting?

- How do you ensure that these are introduced when they are age-/stage-appropriate?

- Do you lend these types of games to parents who may wish to try them at home?

Sorting

Sorting objects into different groups according to shared characteristics provides opportunities for counting and comparing quantities, but also for developing language for thinking. Many children naturally enjoy sorting objects into groups providing that the objects are of interest to them in some way. Commercial sorting sets can be bought, but quite often they are not as appealing to children as real objects that are likely to have more sensory feedback and sorting possibilities.

Using sorting activities with children

Many children will automatically go into sorting mode if the objects available are appealing. The role of the adult is to pick up on the way that children want to sort and sensitively enquire about their reasons for their approach. Some children, for example, will sort according to their 'favourites' or preferences. This is a valid way of sorting, but it might be interesting to see whether children can articulate what makes a certain object or collection 'their favourite'. Adults can also sort objects according to concepts such as colour, size or function alongside children and talk about how they are sorting, so that children can hear their thoughts even if they do not choose to sort in this way.

Setting up sorting activities

It is helpful if sorting is a regular activity for children, but for it to be meaningful there needs to be plenty of variety and the objects themselves need to be appealing. It can also be worth putting out containers to allow for groups of objects to be put into sets, e.g. using small boxes, containers such as muffin tins or even hoops. As children like surprises, try putting objects into gift bags or an attractive box so that they can get pleasure from opening it up and seeing what is there.

Reflection points

- How often are sorting activities planned for children?

- Do you have sufficient collections of interesting materials for children?

- Do you encourage children to find and explain their own way of sorting objects?

- How do you help parents to understand how sorting activities could be used in the home?

Sorting

Objects	Examples	How they may be sorted
Real buttons	• From baby clothes, uniforms, or shirts • Decorative	• Colour • Shape • Function, e.g. buttons for baby clothes • Material, e.g. brass • Fixing method, e.g. two holes, four holes, shanks
Socks	• Baby socks • Sports socks • Novelty socks	• Colour • Length • Purpose • Pattern
Shoes	• Sandals • Boots • Baby shoes • Heels • Clogs	• Colour • Function, e.g. wellington boots, sandals • Length • Fixing, e.g buckle, Velcro, laces
Haberdashery	• Lace • Ribbons • Elastic	• Colour • Length
Jewellery	• Costume jewellery such as necklaces or rings • Brooches made from plastic, with and without stones	• Colour • Length • Function, e.g. rings, necklaces
Locks and keys	• Padlocks • Keys of different sizes • Locks for suitcases	• Function • Size • Type of lock • Matching locks to keys
Toy vehicles	• Cars • Lorries • Vans • Tractors • Trains • Vintage and new • Plastic and metal	• Type of vehicle • Material • Size • Colour • Function

Counting

Children need plenty of experience handling and counting objects, as this is one of the early foundation skills for numeracy. Many people, including parents, underestimate how much practice some children may need before the process of counting and the ability to recognise quantities of five and under becomes automatic. Once children have 'cracked' counting objects one by one, it is helpful for them to see counting modelled in groups of two and also five, as this is a good extension for later numeracy skills.

Role of the adult

Children often pick up the numbers that are said whilst counting because they have heard them modelled by adults. This means that counting aloud during everyday situations is an important role for adults. Adults also have to model how to touch each object as they count. This one-to-one correspondence is important for accurate counting, and it does take a while for children to crack it, even after they have seen it being modelled. As part of the process of learning to count, adults also need to think of counting opportunities that are realistic for children. We may encourage the counting of just three or four objects for a novice 'counter', rather than a boxful. This is important because children do need to feel a measure of success and some children quickly give up when they feel that a task is overwhelming. In the same way, on some occasions, it could be argued that it is better not to correct a child who confidently declares that there are eight dinosaurs when in fact there are only seven.

Why count?

When thinking about counting as a repeated activity, it is important to be child-centred and think carefully about objects and situations where counting will be of interest to children. Are plastic bricks really exciting to count as opposed to seeing if we can find the five dinosaurs asleep in the sand tray? We should also keep an eye on routine 'group' counting that can quickly turn itself into chanting rather than counting accurately. Do children really want to count all the boys then the girls every morning and is this really challenging?

Children learn best when counting and numbers have meaning for them.

Counting

The table below shows some examples of resources and activities that, in my experience, appeal to different children. The key, of course, is to match the counting activity to the interest and personality of the child. It is also useful to make sure that there are opportunities for children to see numbers and to link the numbers to their counting.

Counting resources/activities	Purpose
Ladybirds placed under upturned boxes in the outside area	How many sleeping ladybirds are there living under the boxes?
Dinosaurs hidden in the sand tray	How many dinosaurs have hidden themselves in the sand tray today?
Fake gemstones placed in ice-cube trays	How many jewels does Teddy have?
Shoes in a drawstring fabric bag	How many pairs of shoes has the princess/wizard/giant/(any character known to the child) got?
Plant seeds in a seed tray divided into sections	How many of the seeds have germinated?
Pirate treasure – fake jewellery hidden in the garden	Can you find the treasure that the pirates have hidden? How many items can you find?

Some children like to count with a purpose in mind. This lends itself to setting up playful situations when we might discover how many play cakes Teddy has eaten from the baking tin, or a treasure hunt to find items grouped in threes.

Reflection points

- How many times a session will there be opportunities for interesting counting experiences?

- How do you tailor counting activities to individual children's level of development?

- Do you put out numerals for children to play with, e.g. birthday cards with numbers on them or magnetic numbers?

- How often do you draw children's attention to numerals in a way that interests them?

- Do you help parents look for everyday opportunities to practise counting skills with their children at home?

Measuring

Measuring is a skill that is partly modelled, partly taught and also partly picked up as a result of experience. It is also one of the skills in which adults play an important role in helping learn not only the language of measuring, but also the skills. Whilst many settings do put out measuring jugs, rulers and scales for children to play with, the children who benefit the most are the ones who understand the function of these and have opportunities to measure for a purpose.

Creating opportunities for measuring

Measuring is a tricky skill for children to learn. One of the first steps is for children to learn the varying purposes of measurement, e.g. cooking, seeing if things will fit. This means that adults need to find activities that will appeal to children and be of interest to them. They also need plenty of language opportunities to be able to talk accurately about the process of measuring. Formal measuring, e.g. using standard weights and lengths, can be left for some time as they usually require children to be able to recognise numbers.

Measuring

T!P

Resources/Activities	Purpose
• Three suitcases of different sizes • Selection of clothes	Teddy wants to select the suitcase which all his clothes can fit in to.
• Different lengths of straws pushed into a piece of dough	Can you find the hedgehog's shortest spine?
• Damp sand • Flower pots of different heights	Can you make a sandcastle that is taller than mine?
• Lengths of gift ribbon or string, partially hidden	Can you guess which ribbon is going to be the longest?
• Wrapping paper • Sticky tape • Assorted boxes	Teddy likes opening boxes and presents. How much wrapping paper should I cut?
• Water bottle with mark at half full	This plant only needs to drink half a bottle of water. Can we fill to the halfway mark?
• Balancing scales • Identical gift boxes or bags with different items inside	Teddy wants to have the heaviest present for his birthday.

Children need plenty of practice at measuring.

Reflection points

● How do you help children develop the language associated with measuring?

● During their time with you, how do you ensure that opportunities to measure are varied and also increasingly precise?

● How many cooking activities do you carry out with children that require precise measurement?

Patterns

Recognising and making patterns is a cognitive skill that it is linked to logic. Whilst it is one of those skills that supports numeracy, making and recognising patterns also links to a range of other areas including music, dance and science. Pattern recognition is one of those areas of development where some children find it easier than others to 'see' or 'hear' a pattern. Although we cannot 'fast track' development, we can make sure that children have had opportunities to explore and have their attention draw to patterns.

Helping children to recognise patterns

Most children learn to recognise patterns before going on to make them for themselves. Setting up an environment that has visual patterns in it can be a good starting point. Look out for fabrics, wrapping paper and other objects that have clear patterns on them. Consider laying out resources in simple patterns, e.g. alternating large and small spoons or triangular and square blocks. A good tip is to make sure that patterns are long enough, as some children may only start to see that pattern after some 'distance'. Another tip is to keep the patterns very simple at first.

With different patterns in place, it is also important for children's attention to be drawn to them and thus we might 'narrate' the pattern whilst pointing, e.g. 'A red shoe, a blue shoe, a red shoe, a blue shoe.' We also have to accept that though we might want to draw a child's attention to a pattern, the child might simply want to try the shoes on instead, in which case we will need to focus on this at another time. Luckily, there are many other ways in which we can give children experience of patterns. These include:

- Making necklaces using beads or coloured pasta.

- Putting out toys in a pattern, e.g. red car, blue car, red car…

- Playing clapping games so that children can hear patterns.

- Putting out props in role play areas in a pattern, e.g. large cup, small cup, large cup, small cup…

Threading activities can prompt children to make patterns.

Reflection points

- How do you help children gain an awareness of patterns?

- Do you point out patterns in your environment, e.g. colours of tiles on a wall, spots on fabrics?

- Do you plan activities that will help children recognise and also make patterns?

- How often do you put out objects so that they form a pattern?

Memory games

Though children's memory is linked to development, children can also learn some strategies from adults. Memory games can help children learn some simple strategies whilst also having the advantage of developing children's logic, social skills and even vocabulary. As with all activities, it is important to match the game to the individual children's level of development.

Memory games

There are a wide range of games which children often enjoy playing which include the following:

Pairs	**The game:** Picture cards are put face down. Children have to pick up two cards and see whether the pictures match. If they do not match, children replace the cards. **Potential learning:** Children can learn that putting the cards out in lines and columns makes it easier to find the card that they are looking for.
Kim's game	**The game:** A kitchen tray with ten objects is shown to children. The tray is taken out of sight or covered with a cloth. One object is taken away unseen. Afterwards children have to identify the missing object. **Potential learning:** Children can learn to sort objects into groups, which makes it easier to spot the missing object.
I went to the shops and I bought...	**The game:** Played in a small group, the phrase 'I went to the shops and I bought...' is said with an item added onto the end, e.g. 'a donkey'. The next child then repeats exactly what the previous child said but adds an extra item. **Potential learning:** Children have to listen carefully and memorise what previous children have said and so this is a game that is good for listening, as well as memory skills.

Summary

In this chapter we began by looking at the link between language and cognition. In the context of cognition, we can see how language affects the way that children are able to retain and process information. We have also seen how adults can help children to use language that will help them order their thoughts, predict and reason. We also considered the role of activities that adults might introduce to children to help them to acquire skills, including recognising patterns, sorting and the role that mathematical games can play in helping children practise counting and other mathematical concepts. From this chapter, you might like to reflect on how you develop children's language in relation to thinking, and how you help them to acquire some early mathematical skills.

Chapter 10

Physical development and self-care

When it comes to children at risk of disadvantage and closing the gap, supporting children's physical development and self-care skills must not be overlooked, as they are central to later learning.

Physical development plays a significant role in children's overall development. Being able to sit still, for example, requires that children have sufficient muscle control and can co-ordinate their movements. Whereas in the past, the development of children's physical skills was pretty much taken for granted, today's children have fewer opportunities to practise and develop these skills. Many children have little or no access to a garden so that they can play outdoors, whilst others would prefer to remain indoors and use technology. In addition, opportunities for children to develop self-care skills are not as readily available in some families as they have been in the past. The decline in children's level of fitness and skills has increased the focus on physical development within the early years.

In this chapter, we look at the importance of physical development and self-care skills and ways in which we might support their development.

Role and importance of physical development and self-care skills

One of the reasons why physical development is so important in children's lives is that it acts as a springboard for other areas of development.

Emotional development

Being able to move, co-ordinate actions and show some independence is particularly important for children's sense of efficacy. This is their perception of whether or not they are 'can do' people or whether they see themselves as 'passengers' always needing the support of others. In early childhood, children are still learning about themselves and developing a self-image which is partly drawn from their sense of self-efficacy. It is always interesting to watch children as they acquire new skills and see how their confidence grows.

Physical activity supports children's emotional well-being.

Cognition

Movement appears to play an important role in stimulating the brain in early childhood. This is an ongoing area of research, but there are papers looking at the link between exercise and intelligence. On a practical level, children who are mobile and have developed good hand-eye co-ordination and strength in their hands are able to access more resources and explore the environment in different ways. This in turn allows them increased opportunities to discover, think and process information. A good example of this would be the child who can walk over to a hedge and carefully move a couple of branches in order to look at a bird's nest.

Social skills and play

As children develop, their play and the movements involved in their play become more complex. In the role play area children may pretend to sort out money in a shop, and when using construction toys they might build increasingly complex and fiddly structures. Outdoors, children may run, climb or use wheeled toys as part of their play, or transport water and sand from place to place. Children who have strong levels of physical skills are able to collaborate with others rather than standing on the sideline.

Health

Physical activity has a huge impact on children's health. Weight-bearing movements such as running and walking develop the strength in bones but also having cardiovascular and respiratory benefits. Children's digestion and appetite are also helped by physical activity. In addition, recent research has shown that children who have had exercise fell asleep more quickly and for a longer duration than their counterparts. (Nixon et al, 'Falling asleep: the determinants of sleep latency').

Reflection points

- Does everyone in the team recognise the impact of physical development on other areas of development?

- How are parents helped to understand the importance of physical development to children's overall development and also health?

Observing and assessing children's physical skills

It is important to observe carefully children's physical skills and compare these to age-related milestones, because a delay may be an indicator of an underlying need that will require assessment. This can be anything from a child requiring glasses to a medical condition affecting their co-ordination. To find out what is typical in terms of children's development, it is worth looking at resources such as 'From Birth To Five Years' by Mary Sheridan, or to see if your local NHS physiotherapy team have produced materials. When assessing children, it is important not to make any assumptions about what children can do or have experienced. This is because some children may have gained some skills, but not others because of a lack of resources or opportunities, e.g. a child might be balancing well, but may not have had the opportunity to use a toy involving steering.

In addition, assessing children's physical skills can also help us to plan activities that are within grasp of their skill level. This is important, as children who are repeatedly put in situations when they cannot manage a skill are likely to become frustrated and give up. This can affect their motivation to try out new things or to practise skills.

Reflection points

- Do you observe and assess children's physical skill level in terms of age-related milestones?

- How do you share information with parents about their children's physical skills?

- Do you know where you can find information locally about referring children?

Specific physical skills that children need to acquire

There are a range of physical skills that children need to acquire in order to develop core strength, muscles and co-ordination. It is important to think about whether children have opportunities in the play and activities that you provide to ensure that these skills are developed. In Chapter 8 we looked at ways to strengthen hand preference and also pincer grip.

Core strength

The core muscles are the abdominal muscles that surround the stomach and pelvis. Children will find it hard to sit straight and still for any length of time without strength in these muscles. These muscles are also linked to children's balance. The type of activities that support core strength include:

- Walking

- Running

- Throwing

- Jumping

- Crawling movement, e.g. walking like a monkey, moving like a snake

- Lying on their tummy to play, e.g. using a train set

- Dancing to music

Jumping helps develop children's core strength.

Bilateral co-ordination

This is the skill that allows both sides of the body to work together doing the same movement (e.g. using a rolling pin) or to make alternating movements (e.g. walking). Bilateral movements are also involved when children use two hands, with each hand serving a different purpose (e.g. opening a screw-top bottle). Here are some examples of activities that involve symmetrical and alternate bilateral movements. See Chapter 8, page 146 for examples of two-handed activities where each hand has its own function.

Symmetrical bilateral movements	Alternate bilateral movements
Clapping games	Walking
Beating a drum with two sticks at the same time	Running
Using a sit and ride toy where both feet push down together at the same time	Using a tricycle or pedal toy where each foot takes a turn to push down
Catching a ball with two hands	Using a shaker in each hand, alternating them

Balance

Activities that help children learn to balance also help with core strength and proprioception, the skills associated with knowing where your body is in relation to the ground, other children and space. There are many activities that can support children's balance. They include:

- Wobble boards
- Climbing activities, e.g. walking around a circle of tree stumps
- Stairs and steps
- Walking on uneven surfaces
- Trampolines
- Co-ordinated activities such as walking across the room carrying a spoon with a button in it
- Obstacle courses.

Crossing the midline

The midline is an imaginary line that runs vertically down the centre of the body. The term 'crossing the midline' refers to movements that involve an arm or leg crossing this line, e.g. reaching with the right hand for a toy brick that is on the left hand side, or crossing legs. Movements that involve crossing the midline help children to be more co-ordinated, strengthen hand preference and manage practical tasks such as using a knife and fork. Activities that can help children include:

- Marching movements with hands moving in opposition to the legs
- Crawling movements
- Drawing a rainbow or arc shape whilst kneeling
- Playing games such as 'Simon says...', where children have to make movements such as putting their right hand on their left knee
- Throwing games where a bucket or target is put diagonally opposite the child's throwing hand
- Dancing with scarves.

It takes time for children to learn to co-ordinate their movements.

Hand-eye co-ordination (fine motor)

Many activities require fine motor hand-eye co-ordination. A high level of hand-eye co-ordination is needed for many self-care activities, play and also handwriting. Hand-eye co-ordination is developed through practice so it is important that we look out for activities that increasingly require more accuracy. Activities that require more control may include:

- Dot to dot activities

- Pouring water from a jug into a narrow bottle

- 'Pick-up sticks' or stacking games such as Jenga™

- Sewing and lacing activities

- Using small blocks or Lego™ for construction.

Hand/foot/eye co-ordination – gross motor

Being able to throw, catch, kick and bat requires hands or feet to be co-ordinated in larger movements. These movements develop over time, with catching and batting requiring particularly high levels of skill because they require children to track an oncoming object and position themselves accordingly. As with many areas of physical development, these movements are partly developmental and partly about opportunity. Activities that can help children develop these skills, include:

- Throwing bean bags and eventually aiming at a target

- Catching bubbles or slower moving items, e.g. a ball in a bag

- Catching large soft balls using arms and then hands

- Kicking a large ball – at first stationary and then one that is slowly moving towards them

- Using a bat – at first a bat with a large surface and a slow-moving target, e.g. a balloon.

Building strength in hands

For activities such as holding a pencil or undoing a lid on a bottle, a certain level of strength is needed in the hands. Strength in the hands is partly developmental, but also linked to opportunity.

Activities to help develop hand strength include:

- Undoing bottles

- Peeling fruit

- Grating cheese

- Squeezing water out of sponges

- Using squeezy bottles to squirt water

- Using tweezers and tongs to transport items from one bowl to another.

T!P

Using scissors

Using scissors requires a range of physical skills including strength in hands, hand-eye co-ordination and bilateral movements. I have included it here because children make better progress and become less frustrated when there is a structured approach to it. Most children are not ready to start using scissors until they are aged two and a half or three-years-old. In my work with children, I have found a step-by-step method helpful. This is largely but not exclusively based on the Montessori approach.

Stage 1:

- Work on hand strengthening movements

- Model how to hold the scissors and position the paper – check that scissors are right for the child

- Use thin strips of paper (1 cm width) or dough and encourage children to enjoy snipping

- Add horizontal lines onto the strips of paper for children to line up the scissors and then snip

- As above, but using diagonal lines. Children can then draw their own lines.

Stage 2:

- Use wider strips of paper (3–4 cm). Put a dot in the middle of the strip. See if children can cut to the dot, open the scissors and then finish cutting

- Add horizontal lines to the paper and then see if children want to add and cut on their own lines

- Put a 'V' shape mark onto the strip of paper. See if children can cut to the bottom of the V, open their scissors and turn the paper

- Start introducing shapes with curves onto the strip of paper.

Stage 3: Learning to cut circles

- Practise cutting out circles with dough

- Draw a spiral onto a circle of paper so that children practise cutting round – change the direction of the spiral for children who are left-handed.

It takes time to master cutting with scissors.

Role of rich play provision in supporting children's physical skills

Many opportunities for physical skills should be naturally occurring if the play provision is sufficiently rich. Play is one of the best ways for children to develop physical skills because children tend to naturally repeat movements as part of their play. The key is to make sure that there are sufficient resources available and that children are engaging in a range of enjoyable play types. We also have to ensure that opportunities to increase children's skill level are available, e.g. in the water tray, that there are some narrow necked bottles for children to pour water into or that older children have access to sequins on the collage table.

As some skills require a little modelling or explicit teaching, think about how to incorporate these into play or into an activity that will be highly motivating and enjoyable for a child. Learning how to use scissors, sew or use a grater are examples of these explicit activities.

Reflection points

- How does your planning ensure that specific physical skills and movements are incorporated into play and activities?

- How do you ensure that individual children are making progress in terms of acquiring movements and skills?

- Do you audit your play provision in terms of physical skills?

- How do you ensure that children who are with you for more than one year have opportunities to increase and refine their skill level?

Self-care

There are many self-care skills that children need to develop. With the exception of toileting, they are linked to children's physical development and so working on specific physical skills such as hand-eye co-ordination may be the starting point when looking at how to support children. In this section, I have picked out some key areas of self-care to focus on: toileting, feeding and dressing.

Working with parents

Many of the self-care skills and behaviours need to be practised at home as well as in the early years setting. Therefore, it is important to have a conversation with parents to find out what type of things their child can do at home. Sharing information may be quite revealing, as there will be some children who are being given significant opportunities to show independence beyond those in your setting. In other cases, parents may not know what children of their child's age can typically do and have not thought about providing opportunities. For other parents who may be very aspirational for their children, physical and self-care skills may not be seen as particularly important. It is also not uncommon for some parents to find difficulty in letting the 'baby' of the family grow up. Understanding what parents know and feel about physical and self-care skills is therefore important in order to support them and their child in their 'physical journey'.

Toileting

Being in control over your bodily functions is an important developmental milestone. Children who are not in nappies are able to move more easily, but there are other benefits in terms of self-identity and empowerment. This means that supporting children to move out of nappies is an important area of work within early years settings.

Over the past few years, the age at which children are out of nappies has increased. This is attributed to the effectiveness of disposable nappies. This means that many children who may previously have been out of nappies before their third birthday are still in nappies. There are also reports suggesting that there has been an increase in the number of children entering reception class who are not toilet-trained. There are many issues involved with helping children out of nappies and this is definitely an area where good relationships and agreement with parents can be helpful.

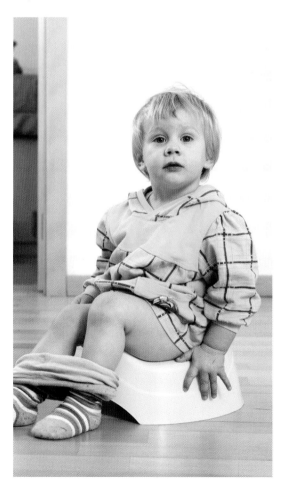

Toilet readiness

Moving out of nappies is first and foremost a developmental process. The key to it being successful is for parents and adults to recognise the signs that a child is ready and then to act fairly promptly. It is helpful to draw up a 'toilet training policy' and a resources pack to facilitate discussions with parents.

Acting promptly

Once children are clearly ready for toilet training, it is important to start the process fairly promptly. Leaving a child in nappies when they could be taking control of their toileting is likely to be demotivating for them in the long run. Effectively, they are learning to be comfortable when they have soiled or wet themselves.

Signs of readiness

For toilet training to be successful, children need a certain level of bladder maturity. They need to be able to retain urine for at least an hour, preferably longer, and then to release it all. When the bladder is not mature, urine is released more as a 'dribble' rather than a 'flood'. This is the starting point and a most important factor in the process. There is no magic age in which children will acquire this maturity and the age span can be huge. Some children are out of nappies at eighteen months, others will be closer to three years.

As well as bladder maturity, children also need to become aware that they are passing urine. Putting children into less efficient nappies or lining them with kitchen paper can help children make the link between the act of urination and feeling wet. In addition, when adults spot that children are passing a stool or have stopped in their tracks to pass urine, they should comment on the process, e.g. 'Josh, your wee is coming out. Let's get you clean now'. It is also important for nappies to be promptly changed so that children learn to feel good about being clean.

Patience

Once children are ready, the next step is for them to be introduced to the potty with minimum fuss. On the first day, it can be worth reminding children to try after an hour or so when you know that there will be sufficient urine. Making children sit and 'try' every fifteen minutes or so tends to result in the child becoming frustrated and losing confidence because there may not be anything to produce. The key is to be patient and expect a few accidents. Although some children are quick to develop an association, others will be slower. Any pressure put onto the child is likely to backfire, even if the child is told that they can have a reward. This is because in order to release urine, the muscles around the bladder have to relax. Children who are stressed in anyway are likely to find this difficult. For most children who show bladder maturity, toilet training should take about a week or so with the child gradually becoming more competent.

Why children have accidents

During and even after toilet training, it is important that adults realise that children's bladders send out signals when there is pretty much no capacity left. (This is different to adults' bladders that first send signals at the halfway mark.) In practical terms, this means that a child probably has five or at best just ten minutes to get themselves to the toilet. Making children wait or not having easy access to toilets or potties therefore increases the risks of accidents within the setting as well as the risk of urinary infections.

For some children, accidents occur because they are distracted by what they are doing and so do not register their bladder's signal. There are also some children who have not learnt for themselves what a full bladder feels like. This may be because adults have always reminded them to go before the bladder has had a chance to send out signals. If this is the case, the trick is to cut out the reminders or to ask children to stop and think about what they are feeling.

Constipation

There has been an increase in the number of children who are constipated and this causes a range of difficulties. Firstly, some children may prefer to wet themselves rather than go to the toilet. This is because they know that otherwise they may pass a stool and this will be painful. For other children, constipation results in a combination of diarrhoea or soiling that they cannot control.

Once a child has experienced constipation, they can develop a fear of toilets and so may refuse to come out of nappies. For some children constipation is caused by poor diet or insufficient hydration, whilst for others it is linked to too much pressure during the toilet training process. As constipation can really affect children's emotional well-being as well as health, it is important to encourage parents to seek help early rather than later on.

Additional support

Toilet training and issues such as constipation can be surprisingly tricky. It is therefore worth knowing where you and parents can get support locally. This may include health visitors and clinics. In addition, there are useful articles on the internet including the NHS Live Well website (www.nhs.uk/livewell). For more detailed information about potty training and also bedwetting, consider ERIC, the children's continence charity's website (www.eric.org.uk).

Reflection points

- How do you work with parents to help them through the toilet training process?

- Do you have resources or a 'toilet training' pack for parents?

- Does everyone understand the importance of recognising the signs of toilet readiness?

- Are attractive toiles and potties readily available?

Feeding

Learning to be independent at meal and snack times is an important self-care skill. As with other self-care skills, it is linked both to development and also opportunities to practise. It is another confidence booster for children to be able to take care of themselves and so it is important to work alongside parents to look for opportunities to support them.

Cultural expectations

One of the key differences between many families is the way in which meals and snacks take place. For some families normality is a table, whilst for others it is the floor. For some families mealtimes are social gatherings, but for others eating alone or in front of a television is the norm. In some homes, no one starts eating before everyone is there or leaves until everyone has finished. In others, there is in effect a 'rolling mealtime'. The dishes, cutlery and customs about how to eat can also be very different, as might the expectations of children at mealtimes. This means that a good starting point is to find out from parents what their children are used to doing. This will help you to work out (preferably with the parents) what support individual children will need in order to take part in the mealtimes and snack times in your setting.

Developmental expectations

With early years settings increasingly taking children from two-years-old, it can be helpful to be aware of typical developmental milestones for feeding skills. Using these can help to ensure that your expectations and the way that you organise mealtimes are developmentally realistic.

18–24 months	• Chews with lips closed • Cup now placed between lips rather than teeth • Able to load spoon and take to mouth without spilling
2–2 ½ years	• Holds cup in one hand • Uses spoon independently
2 ½–3 years	• Uses spoon independently • From 30 months starts to use spoon and fork with adult grip • May become fussy or show clear food preferences
3–3 ½ years	• Pours water from a jug into a cup
3 ½–4 years	• Uses a spoon and fork well and is starting to use a knife at times • Can spread butter onto bread with a knife
4–4 ½ years	• Can use knife and fork competently

Organising mealtimes and snack times

For some children, the way that your meals and snacks are organised will be new to them as well as the accompanying expectations. This means that modelling and also patience will be needed as children take their time to adjust. Visual step-by-step guides can also help children to understand what they need to do, e.g. take their plate over to the sink when finished. In addition, we need to make sure that resources such as spoons are age-/stage-appropriate and that tables are at the right height for children. Observing children closely and changing utensils, if necessary, can help children to learn new skills, e.g. a bowl is easier to use with a fork and spoon rather than a plate.

It is also important that enough time is given, as very young children are notoriously slow eaters and sometimes they are best off in very small groups as they are more easily distracted from the task in hand.

Increasing challenge

As children develop, we also need to think about increasing the level of physical challenge. It may be that once they have eaten, they can wash and dry their own plate or that they are involved in the preparation of the meal or snack.

Reflection points

- Are resources and furniture for feeding age-/stage-appropriate?

- Are expectations realistic for children's age and experience?

- Is enough time given for children to feed themselves?

- Does the play environment provide opportunities for children to practise the skills needed at meal times, e.g. pouring, using a spoon?

- Are children increasingly given more opportunities to become involved in the preparation of snacks and mealtimes?

- What information do you share about children's progress in your setting?

Dressing

Learning to dress helps children to gain independence and also helps in terms of toileting. It takes a range of skills including balance and hand-eye co-ordination. As with feeding, it is important to have realistic expectations of children to avoid situations where children lose confidence or become frustrated. Interestingly, the process of learning to dress usually begins with a child undressing. Time also matters, as children need to develop co-ordination and sequencing skills and young children are notoriously slow at getting dressed, especially if there are any distractions. This is often one reason why parents and other adults tend to take over from children, especially if they are in a rush.

Age-related expectations

Knowing what children can typically do at any given age can be useful so you can judge whether your expectations are realistic and also as an aid for planning.

2 years	• Can remove shoes and socks • Can pull on simple clothing such as T-shirts, but will need help to find arms • Can pull up and push down underpants, trousers and socks, but not step into them
2 ½ years	• Tries to put short socks on although may need help putting the heel in place • Can unbutton clothing with large buttons • Can put on coats, but not yet fasten them
3 years	• Able to put on a T-shirt with minimal help • Can put on shoes, but may not differentiate right from left • Can put on socks with minimal help • Can pull up trousers and may attempt to put them on with varying success
3 ½ years	• Able to unzip jacket and pull shank at bottom apart • Can unbutton large buttons at front • Able to find the front of clothing and put on many items, e.g. jumpers, T-shirts • Can put on trousers but may need assistance
4 years	• Able to dress fairly well, but will still need assistance with small buttons or zips at times.
5 years	• Able to dress independently

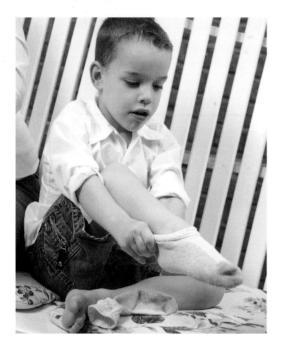

Learning to dress takes practice as well as encouragement from adults.

Reflection points

- Do you give children sufficient time to manage dressing tasks?

- Do you recognise when children need support and provide it promptly?

- Do you guide children with step-by-step instructions so that they learn the process?

- Do you and other adults have realistic expectations of children's dressing?

- Do you ensure that children have space and few distractions when they need to dress?

- Do you plan activities or have resources that will support dressing skills, e.g. a range of fabric bags that toys can be put inside but which have zips or buttons to open them?

- Do you help children to identify the front and back of clothes, e.g. looking for the label in the back?

Nose blowing

Many children are not able to blow their nose. This is because it is hard for them to follow adult's instructions. Instead many will just wipe their noses because they do not connect the word 'blow' with air being pushed down the nose. A useful tip is to work on this skill before a child has a cold. By rolling up a small ball of tissue paper and putting it on the table, see if children can make it move by blowing air through their noses alone. You may need to remind children to keep their mouths closed whilst they are doing this. The idea is that once they have done this several times, they can associate the feeling of blowing through their nose with the phrase 'blow your nose'!

Hand washing

Learning to wash your hands and knowing when to do it helps cut down on infections and also cross infections. For some children, hand washing takes place regularly at home, but for others it may be a skill that they will need to be taught. It is helpful if children are able to copy an adult's hand washing technique and for the adult to narrate what they are doing step-by-step. To properly wash, rinse and dry hands, takes some time, so it is useful to make this a fun activity by making up a hand washing song. We may also need to think about whether children will skimp on hand washing because they are afraid that they will miss out on a more interesting activity.

Role of routines to support self-care and life skills

All self-care activities, including washing hands, need to be frequently practised by children in order that they can master them. It is therefore important to build self-care skills into the routine of the setting and also look for opportunities to teach children new life skills, such as using a dustpan and brush, laying a table or drying up a cup. Many self-care and life skills are also great opportunities for adult-child interaction, as well as ways to reinforce physical skills. It is therefore important to make sure that they are seen as purposeful learning experiences in their own right rather than activities to speed through.

Reflection points

- Does everyone in the setting model good handwashing?

- Is the hand washing area attractive?

- Can children reach the washbasin and the taps?

- Do you have a visual step-by-step guide to remind children how to wash their hands?

- Do you have a hand washing song?

- Do you remind children about when to wash their hands and praise them afterwards?

Reflection points

- Do you have a list of self-care skills that forms part of your education programme and planning?

- Does everyone in the setting understand the learning opportunities and importance of self-care and life skills?

- How do you communicate and celebrate with parents the value of self-care skills?

Summary

In this chapter, we have looked at the importance of physical development and self-care skills as part of children's overall development especially in relation to their sense of self and cognition. We have seen that children need to develop a wide range of physical skills and that these might need to be planned for as they may not always develop by chance. We have also seen that self-care skills are also part of children's early years journey and that adults need to have realistic expectations as well as strategies to promote these. Following this chapter, you may like to think about how your setting strategically promotes not only physical movements, but also self-care skills.

A final word

Even though the issues around educational disadvantage and social mobility are complex, I firmly believe that it is possible, with vision and strategic planning, for early years settings to make a significant impact on children's lives. It is after all, what many of us came into this sector to do!

Throughout this book, I have tried to pinpoint strategies and ideas that you may find helpful when planning your own next steps for the children in your setting. As every setting is different and the needs of children will vary, it is important to take time to develop your own vision and action plan in relation to the topics within this book.

There are three key themes in particular that run throughout this book which you may have noticed and which I believe are worth reflecting on in your practice.

The role of the adult

Throughout this book we have seen that the role of the adult, be it parents or practitioners, can impact significantly on children's development. Although this is of course nothing new, I would ask all settings to think carefully about how they engage with parents and how they deploy staff or their own time. We know, for example, that high-quality, enjoyable and carefully chosen adult-directed activities can have a huge impact on children's learning. These include, for example, shared stories as well as mathematical games. We also know that children benefit hugely where adults become involved sensitively in their play. It is therefore important that all settings take stock of how adults, a significant resource, are being used to support children.

Taking the long view

Another emerging theme within this book is the need for long-term and strategic planning. In many ways this goes against the current trend of exclusively planning day-by-day or week-by-week and basing everything around children's interests. This is a theme that you might like to take time to reflect on and one that might provoke some interesting comments and debates amongst your colleagues. In particular, I would urge you to consider whether you need to take a planned approach towards outings, visitors and even simple activities such as cooking and gardening.

The importance of developing children's language

Finally, another key theme throughout this book is the role that adults, including parents, can play in developing children's language. We have seen that in some of the key areas that will impact on children's future learning, including literacy and mathematics, strong levels of language are needed. We have also seen how language impacts on children's social skills and self-regulation. To make a difference to children at risk of disadvantage, how we support children's language across all areas of the curriculum needs to be at the forefront of our practice.